For Such a Time as This: Aligning Church and Leadership for Missional Ministry

Ircel Harrison

Pinnacle Leadership Press

www.pinnaclelead.com

Dedicated to
my grandchildren and great-grandchildren
and the church they will create
in partnership with the Spirit of God

Foreword

The keynote speaker at a conference for Christian scholars that I recently attended addressed a topic of interest to all of the participants. She spoke at length about the history of Christianity and claimed that we are currently in a period of intense change when it comes to thinking about church. If the church is to remain relevant, she asserted, it must be transformed. She cited the emergent church as one example of how the church is changing with little comment about change in traditional or mainline churches.

Any Christian following the news has heard similar information. Mainline denominations or traditional churches are in decline, and "nones" (or the religiously unaffiliated) are growing at a rapid pace, especially among those who are under thirty years of age. Members of this group oftentimes describe themselves as spiritual but not religious and are not searching for a religious home. The rapid growth of this demographic is indicative of the change facing the church.

In *For Such a Time as This: Aligning Church and Leadership for Missional Ministry*, Ircel Harrison provides us with an alternative and necessary perspective for thinking about the church of today and the church of the future. Sharing with the reader the importance of considering what it means to be a missional church, Harrison argues that, "missional ecclesiology reframes the way we see who we are and what we are about."

Rather than settling down to watch as the number of "nones" continues to increase or accept the idea that the emergent church is the only type of church that will survive in years to come, Harrison encourages those in traditional churches to think of the opportunities that might be revealed if a missional ecclesiology were adopted. What would it mean to spend serious time discerning how God wants us to be in the world and how we might carry out the work of Christ in our contexts? Traditional churches have the opportunity to be transformed and to be relevant actors in the Christianity of the future.

Harrison is uniquely qualified to share this hopeful and encouraging vision. Having spent the majority of his life in traditional churches, he has also served in various leadership roles within the church and at the denominational level from pastor to coordinator of the Tennessee Cooperative Baptist Fellowship. His training in leadership and coaching adds another substantive dimension to his work, and more than anything, his love of the church is communicated powerfully throughout this text.

This is a visionary work and one that all who are interested in the future of the church should read. The content also would be helpful to any organization interested in addressing the idea of what it means to be a community and to be in community. It is an essential read for all Christians interested in the effectiveness of and future of the church.

Dr. Sally Holt
Professor of Religion, Belmont University
Site Director, Central Baptist Theological Seminary Tennessee

Table of Contents

Foreword

Section One: Starting Where You Are   1

    Chapter One: Images of the Church   3

    Chapter Two: New Wineskins   11

    Chapter Three: The Challenge of Change   19

    Chapter Four: Becoming Missional   31

Section Two: Leadership Lessons   41

    Chapter Five: What Kind of Leaders Does the   45
    Missional Church Need?

    Chapter Six: Discovering Your Calling   59

    Chapter Seven: Leading in the 21st Century   65

    Chapter Eight: Developing an Effective Leadership   77
    Team

Afterword: Will We Know the Future When We See It?   85

After the Afterword   89

Endnotes   91

Bibliography   95

Endorsements   97

Section One

Starting Where You Are

Perhaps one of the greatest and simplest inventions of the last century was the map at the mall with the dot marking the spot where you are standing when you read the map: "You are here." On one occasion I thought, "Where else would I be?" But it does make sense, doesn't it? We must start where we are geographically, in time, in life, and in leadership of the church. It would be foolish to start where you are not!

A number of outstanding books have been written over the last two decades about the missional church—a church that is "on mission with God" or acknowledges that it is part of the *missio Dei*. The most creative yet less helpful ones are those that assume that you are either starting a church from scratch or that you are willing to commit ministerial suicide by instituting radical change in an established church in order for it to become missional.

The most helpful volumes are written for those who lead traditional churches that have plateaued, are declining, are seeing a new understanding of what it means to be the church, or lack spiritual vitality.[1] These books acknowledge that members expect pastoral care; you have to subscribe

> *Whether a church can ever be a truly "missional church" is debatable, but becoming one is a worthy goal and one that any church can work toward if it decides to begin that journey.*

an annual budget; your church building may need repairs; established constituencies exist within the congregation built on certain interests—music, youth, missions, and so on; and that you are dealing with a leadership body you did not select—church council, deacons, session, or parish council.

I have been a part of such churches most of my life. I participated in one new church start that survived and worked on another that didn't, but both were rather traditional in their approach to "doing church." Therefore, when I write about the church, I am coming out of an established church tradition. At the same time, I believe that it is possible for such churches to embark on the journey of "becoming missional." Whether a church can ever be a truly "missional church" is debatable, but becoming one is a worthy goal and one that any church can work toward if it decides to begin that journey.

I love the church, but I recognize that it is led by and composed of individuals. These persons have accepted the call to be the people of God, but they are still flawed, seeking individuals. As I address issues related to the missional journey, I hope my readers will understand that I appreciate the daily challenges involved in "becoming missional" but also realize the great hope it gives to each congregation. We look to the stars, but our feet are planted firmly on the ground.

Chapter One

Images of the Church

What comes to mind when you think of "church"? A group of people? A physical location? A biblical concept? Many ideas and images characterize the church, some rooted in Scripture and some in culture. Perhaps the best place to start is in the Bible. In *Coming Together in the 21st Century: The Bible's Message in an Age of Diversity*[2], Curtiss Paul DeYoung provides several images of community found in the Bible and gives a good starting point for understanding "church."

Church as Contrast Community

What is your image of "community"? This means different things to each of us, but few would deny that community is meant to be embodied within the church. Not only is true community at the heart of the Christian life (and our Trinitarian

3

theology), but healthy community is necessary for all human growth and spiritual development.

One of the recurring themes in missional theology is the idea of church as

Healthy community is necessary for all human growth and spiritual development.

"contrast community." Although I first heard this phrase used in regard to the missional church, DeYoung points out that the Hebrew Bible first introduced the concept to describe God's desire for the nation of Israel. God intended for the people of God to offer an alternative or contrast to the ways of other nations. He writes, "The laws given in Exodus, Leviticus, and Deuteronomy emphasized social justice and human relations. . . . The contrast community implies that for community to flourish, it must integrate equality and justice into the formation of its organizational principles and ways of daily living."[3] He concludes, however, that this was an ideal that was never fully actualized in the life of the Israelites once they entered Palestine.

What implications does this suggest for the church seeking to practice community today? We could quickly jump to the need to provide a contrast to society in our practices of justice and social equality, but I suggest that we look inward rather than outward for our critique. Our society (and the

Does the church exemplify humankind at its best or worst?

motivation may be economic rather than altruistic) has done more to promote equality and justice than many of our churches have.

Can a church that struggles with issues of gender and racial acceptance really be a Christian community? If we deny places of leadership to gifted women and look suspiciously at those of other races who worship with us, are we living up to God's clear expectations for God's people? Does the church exemplify humankind at its best or its worst? What do you think?

Church as *Koinonia*

One of the major challenges facing most churches today is that members really do not know each other. They have little in common in their daily lives or in the church. They no longer live in proximity with one another or cross paths daily. Many people commute long distances to work and may even commute to their church on the weekend. When they come to worship, they often participate as spectators in a service others lead and then leave as quickly as possible. Neither daily life nor the church offers community cohesion.

DeYoung provides the biblical image of the church as *koinonia*, the Greek word for "fellowship," "participation," or "communion." He writes, "The biblical image of koinonia epitomizes a quality of fellowship that encourages participation and togetherness linked in a common cause."[4] He uses the church at Jerusalem (Acts 2:44-47; 4:32-35) as an example of the church functioning in this way.

DeYoung comments that, "This passage [sic] informs us that true community is possible only when there is sacrifice and substantial sharing."[5] He goes on to observe that many Christians today are so selfish that they cannot conceive of sharing economic resources as the will of God. For me, the amazing part is that these people knew each other well enough to know who was in need!

True *koinonia* comes in two ways—through the investment of time getting to know one another and as the gift of God. As believers spend time together sharing their stories—their struggles, their needs, their defeats, and their victories—they come to discern the Spirit of God working in their midst. We can set the stage for koinonia to be created but the gift will only come when God

> *We can set the stage for koinonia to be created but the gift will only come when God provides it.*

provides it. This type of fellowship is rooted in our individual relationship with Christ as well as our individual commitment to one another. The horizontal relationship with other believers is born out of our vertical relationship with God.

In an age of instant gratification, are we willing to take the time for *koinonia*?

Church as Household of God

One of the most powerful images of the church that DeYoung highlights is the church as the household of God. The phrase is found in 1 Peter 4:17, Galatians 6:10, and Ephesians 2:19. In Ephesians 2:19-20, we read: "Consequently, you are no longer foreigners and aliens, but fellow citizens with God's people and members of God's household, built on the foundation of the apostles and prophets, with Christ Jesus himself as the chief cornerstone."

"Household of God" may be a more powerful image than "family of God" for believers. The home was the center of life in Jesus' day. Very often the economic as well as the social lives of family members were centered in the home as family members had particular responsibilities in a family business. They understood their roles and accepted their responsibilities. Everyone had a place in the household and a contribution to make.

> *"Household of God" may be a more powerful image than "family of God" for believers.*

This is a great example of cooperation, one that we need in the church today. A church in our area has chosen to reach out to other parts of the world to start new congregations. Their strategy is to put together teams of church members who will relocate to another part of the world to plant a new church. This is a long-term investment that requires them to give up their lives here and become part of the new culture. One team will soon leave for an Asian country and another is preparing to go to a European country. The genius of the plan is that they are spending their time prior to departure in studying, planning, and praying together. They are getting to know each other's strengths, needs, and skills. They will truly be a family, a household of God, before they leave on their mission. When they begin the tough job of church planting, they will know how to support and help each other.

This is the way a church ought to operate. In the church, we should come to know each other's strengths and needs, acknowledging our dependence on God to provide the mission, priorities, and structure for the work. We can become what God has called us to be in this household because God is the founder and guide.

Church as Table Fellowship

Growing up as a Baptist in the south, "dinner on the grounds" was practically the third ordinance of the church after Baptism and the Lord's Supper. In fact, most of us considered Baptist potlucks as a continuation of the Lord's Supper. How wrong we were because we usually confined our table fellowship to those like ourselves. Jesus practiced a different standard both in those he selected as dinner partners and in the institution of the Lord's Supper (or Communion).

> *By breaking bread together, we were not only nourishing our bodies but our souls as well.*

The final biblical image of the church DeYoung presents is table fellowship. Jesus was notorious for inviting anyone to the table where he was eating, whether he was the host or someone else was (Mark 2:15-16 and Luke 15:2, for example). DeYoung points out that "Jesus even shared a table with Judas, who was preparing to betray him in a few hours."[6] From a theological perspective, Jesus even saw table fellowship as a sign of the kingdom (Luke 14:15-24; 16:19-31).

Many of us remember not only the days when African-Americans and Euro-Americans did not sit down at the dinner table together, but we also remember the first time we broke

7

through that barrier. For many of us, it happened within the context of Christian fellowship. By breaking bread together, we were not only nourishing our bodies but our souls as well. We were acknowledging our relationship to those who were our brothers and sisters and from whom we had been separated for too long.

> *Does your image of the church hinder you from doing what God has called you to do?*

Whether it is the dinner table, the café table at Starbucks, or the Lord's Table of Communion, we must welcome everyone if the church is to be true to the desires of its Master. Jesus was ready to sit down with anyone. Are we?

What's Your Paradigm for Church?

A paradigm is a way of perceiving reality, the way we look at things. Our paradigms are ingrained so deeply that we rarely notice them. Paradigms give structure but they can also limit us. The image of church that we embrace is a paradigm—a way of perceiving reality that determines the questions we ask, what we value, and the way we act. Does your image of the church hinder you from doing what God has called you to do? If so, perhaps it is time to discover a new way of looking at the church.

Questions for Reflection and Discussion

1. What is the most difficult part of being a "contrast community"?

2. How does your church recognize and minister to members in need?

3. In your church fellowship, where do you have the opportunity to learn about each other's gifts and strengths?

4. How often do you share a meal with someone of a different race or ethnic background?

5. If your church were to select one of these images to describe itself (Contrast Community, *Koinonia*, Household of God, Table Fellowship) what would it be?

6. What are some images or metaphors that you might identify to describe the church?

Chapter Two
New Wineskins

When we think of "church," we often think "congregation": building, people, location, programs. This is the traditional faith community that most of us experience. A new model is emerging, however. This model has been called many things, but I refer to it as the "missional faith community."

In *Missional Renaissance*, Reggie McNeal introduces such groups in this way: "The anticipated future has arrived in the form of missional communities in every culture where the Westernized Constantinian order is collapsing and the organic church is taking root."[7] I won't try to unpack everything that McNeal is saying there, but the key point is this: A more incarnational form is replacing the institutional form of the church.

These groups go by several names. In Europe, they are called "clusters" or "midsized groups." The model includes many of the groups that we would call "house churches."

Some take the form of "new monastic communities." Whatever they are called, they tend to have four characteristics in common.

First, they are committed to the **spiritual growth** of the participants. They encourage one another in spiritual formation and the practice of the disciplines of the faith.

A more incarnational form is replacing the institutional form of the church.

Second, they are engaged in **ministry in the world**. They may be focused on being the presence of Christ in their neighborhood, their workplaces, or in a common ministry that all members of the group support.

Third, they **create community and practice hospitality**. They are committed to one another but not at the expense of the guests in their fellowship.

Fourth, they practice **accountability.** They believe that genuine spiritual growth and authentic ministry only take place where there is a high degree of accountability.

Are these churches? Yes and no. I suppose it depends on your definition of church. They certainly are expressions of the people of God on mission with God. If that is what you mean by church, yes. They are not concerned about buildings, programs, and building an institution. But if that is what you mean by church, no.

What is the relationship of missional faith communities to the traditional church? What lessons can we learn from these communities that might transform traditional congregations?

Spiritual Growth

Where does spiritual growth take place? If your immediate response is "the church," please think again. Where have your most meaningful spiritual experiences taken place? I am sure that we would all mention times of worship, Sunday school classes, retreats, and other church-based activities, but we would also talk about one-on-one conversations with friends, an "Aha!" moment in Bible reading, a time of quiet contemplation on the beach or along a mountain trail, an awareness of blessedness in family life, or a sudden realization of answered (or unanswered) prayer as we drove to work.

> *Missional faith communities lend themselves to this "customized" approach to spiritual growth.*

As Reggie McNeal comments in *Missional Renaissance*, many of us (especially in the West) have come to the conclusion that the church can "provide the venues and opportunities for people to live out their entire spiritual journey as part of a church-sponsored or church-operated activity."[8] This assumes that what is spiritual takes place within the walls of the church and not in the world. He goes on to say, "Everyday living is where spiritual development is worked out."[9]

Spiritual growth is not done as part of a production schedule or an assembly line. Each person is so unique in the eyes of God that we must recognize that our spiritual journeys may have a common thread but the final product may be a surprise. Missional faith communities lend themselves to this "customized" approach to spiritual growth.

One of the characteristics of missional faith communities is that they are committed to the spiritual growth of their participants. Members of these communities encourage one another in spiritual formation and the practice of the disciplines of the faith. They allow time and space for members not only to learn but to learn at their own pace. This learning may well involve mentoring and coaching experiences that are not available in larger groups. They also take seriously what members are discovering about their walk with God through their lives in the marketplace and service in the larger community.

Certainly spiritual growth does take place in the programs and activities of the church, but the Spirit moves far beyond those walls.

Ministry in the World

In recent years, I have become aware of people in our congregation who have significant ministries in the community—the lawyer who volunteers with the domestic violence center, the former heart patient who spends time each week visiting heart patients and sharing insights about how to live with their disease, the busy mother who tutors at-risk children, the business person who finds himself the "chaplain" in his workplace. This is what missional Christians do; they serve in the world. These are not church-sponsored activities. These are ministries they have identified and pursued.

The challenge for the church is to give members the permission to seek out and pursue their ministries in the world.

In *Missional Renaissance*, Reggie McNeal notes: "People don't *go* to church; they *are* the church. They don't bring people to church; they bring the church to people."[10] Wherever a believer is, there the church is present. For some reason, we have erected an artificial dividing line between "sanctioned" and "unsanctioned" ministry.

The challenge for the church is to give members the permission to seek out and pursue their ministries in the world. We value what people do within the walls of the church through recognition, training, and encouragement, but we fail to do that for those who are doing Kingdom work outside the walls. In fact, we sometimes make members feel guilty if they are using their gifts elsewhere! The traditional church needs to find ways to bless and commission those who undertake ministries in the larger community.

Let us remember that God is always at work in the world and invites us to join in that activity.

Missional faith communities, on the other hand, start out with this approach as a basic premise. They expect their members to be engaged in ministry in the world. They may be focused on being the presence of Christ in their neighborhood, their workplaces, or in a common ministry that all members of the group support. Very often, missional faith communities form around a particular ministry or a specific neighborhood in order to make a difference there.

Let us remember that God is always at work in the world and invites us to join in that activity. Whether we are part of a traditional congregation or a missional faith community, we are called to an external ministry focus.

Hospitality

I have been told that wait staff in restaurants are not particularly happy to see church folks after Sunday morning worship. They often find the "brothers and sisters" demanding, rude, and lousy tippers! I am sure that not all believers are like this (I try to smile and leave appropriate tips), but this does remind us how important first impressions are.

Genesis 14 offers an interesting story about first impressions involving Abram (Abraham) and Melchizedek, the king of Salem and a "priest of God Most High" (v. 18). As Abraham returned victorious from a battle, Melchizedek brought out bread and wine and blessed Abraham. In response to this show of hospitality, Abraham gave him a tenth of the spoils of the victory.

> We must be aware of the needs of others as well as the possibility of their blessing us.

The story's impact comes not only from the act of hospitality on the part of Melchizedek, but the response of Abraham. The king of Salem was "the other." He was neither part of Abraham's family nor one of his friends. He was, however, a holy man and a "priest of God Most High." He welcomed Abraham, cared for him, and blessed him. Abraham responded with openness and gratitude. Subsequently, this type of hospitality was expected among the Hebrew people.

15

The Old Testament Scriptures repeatedly direct them to show hospitality for "the stranger within their gates."

Christians must also show hospitality to those both within and outside of the church. We must be aware of the needs of others as well as the possibility of their blessing us. For example, although we have come a long way in race relations in our country, it is rare to see African-Americans in a white church and vice versa.

> *Living in community requires not only boundaries but a social contract as well.*

Missional faith communities are very intentional about creating community and practicing hospitality. They are committed to one another but not at the expense of "the other" who is different in some significant way. In fact, missional faith communities go out of their way to embrace those who are different. In so doing, they may well be blessed.

No one said being missional was easy!

Accountability

We've all heard it—usually from a child about 5 or 6 years old but the malady may continue into the teen years: "You're not my boss!" We learn to assert independence (and defiance) at an early age. As we discover our personal autonomy, we feel compelled to express it.

We see this quite often in our daily lives—at work, at sporting events, in the church. The autonomous individual must exercise his or her free will no matter the consequences. I certainly agree that each of us is free to make our own decisions but this freedom must be balanced with responsibility and accountability. Living in community requires not only boundaries but a social contract as well. In return for our autonomy, we must be willing to give up some things. In doing so, we become not only moral beings but responsible members of society. This is the way that leads to growth.

16

In *Missional Renaissance*, Reggie McNeal writes, "Genuine spirituality lives and flourishes only in cultures and relationships of accountability."[11] Churches fail their members when they do not help them become intentional about their own growth and provide structures to help them in their development. This is not authoritarianism. This is a personal responsibility but others can help the disciple in his or her growth.

[*Missional faith communities practice accountability.*]

Being part of a small group and becoming accountable to that group as one develops in spiritual disciplines such as centering prayer and fasting encourages one to practice new habits of faith. A similar emphasis is found in coaching. Life coaches provide accountability to their clients but they have only the authority given to them by the clients themselves.

Missional faith communities practice accountability. They believe that genuine spiritual growth and authentic ministry only take place where a high degree of accountability exists. Because of their size, this is a very intentional and visible part of their community life. Whether the accountability is to the entire group or to another individual, the member of a missional faith community is deeply involved in his or her own spiritual development. Each person knows that others not only will hold them accountable but will provide support and guidance as well.

Is this counter-cultural? It probably is, but maybe that is why it is so important.

Transitioning

Although not every believer is called to be part of a missional faith community, each of us has the opportunity to be part of a missional church. We can learn much from these intentional communities about spiritual growth, ministry in the world, hospitality, and accountability. What we learn can challenge our traditional churches to move to another level of mission.

Try this experiment. Find a rubber band. Loop one end around the fingers of your left hand and the other end around the fingers of your right hand. Now pull your hands apart until you start to feel some resistance. The trick is to build some tension without breaking the rubber band. This is the challenge of creating a mindset for a traditional church to become more missional. You want a bit of tension but you don't want to break the fellowship.

As we consider becoming more missional in future chapters, keep in the mind the challenge of moving toward a new way of doing church without breaking the bands of fellowship.

Questions for Reflection and Discussion

1. Does your congregation display the characteristics of a missional faith community? What are they?

2. How does your congregation encourage members to become externally focused in ministry?

3. How do you respond to McNeal's statement, "Genuine spirituality lives and flourishes only in cultures and relationships of accountability"? Is this true in your experience? What are the accountability structures in your church that encourage growth in spirituality?"

4. What strategies might you adopt to provide relationships of accountability that promote discipleship growth?

Chapter Three
The Challenge of Change

Change is rarely a popular topic but to live is to change. William Bridges wrote that it is not that people don't like change; they just don't like being changed! In order for a church to become more missional, the people and the leaders must be willing not only to address the topic of change but to experience it as well.

Knowing When to Change

In *Great by Choice*, Jim Collins and Morten Hansen make this observation: "Conventional wisdom says that change is hard. But if change is so difficult, why do we see more evidence of radical change in the less successful comparison cases [in the research study]? Because change is *not* the most difficult part. Far more difficult than implementing change is figuring out what works, understanding why it works, grasping when to change, and knowing when not to."[12]

This is a significant finding and one those of us in the church should reflect on! We realize that change is necessary at times, especially if something is no longer effective. Too often we spend time propping up things no one really wants to support. But if something is basically sound, productive, and has a committed core of support, we should not rush to change it.

> *We don't need to continue those things that have outlived their usefulness and in which people are no longer invested.*

A pastor friend once proposed that his church cease Sunday night services because only a few people attended and the service required several hours of staff preparation each week. A delegation of upset church members visited him, urging that the service continue. He asked the group, "Will you come regularly if we continue this service?" The consensus reply was, "We can't make that kind of commitment." The pastor then asked, "Then why should we do this service?" One person summed up the group's attitude: "Well, we just want to know that it's there if we decide to come."

We don't need to continue those things that have outlived their usefulness and in which people are no longer invested. This is not a matter of numbers but of effectiveness. There are things that are going well in our churches and some that would go even better if we tweaked them a bit. Adjustments in time, leadership, format, or preparation could make a great difference.

Perhaps the key question is, "Is this building up the kingdom of God?" If the answer is "No," it is time to change. If the answer is "Yes," let's get on with it and do it well.

Deep Roots

If change is to happen in a congregation, the starting place is spiritual and relational vitality.[13] Change will provoke resistance, disagreement, and even anger, so it is important that congregants have the kind of relationships and spiritual commitment that will allow members to overcome those responses and emerge as a healthy and committed fellowship.

Spiritual and relational vitality provide the strong root system that supports change. Those who work with trees tell me that the root system of a tree below ground is as massive as the spread of the branches above ground. If the root system is not healthy, it cannot support an expanding, growing plant.

We had a particularly dry summer one year. I did not think too much about how it affected the trees around our house until we had a couple of windstorms and lost large branches on several trees. The roots had inadequate nourishment, so the trees had been weakened. Even though the branches grew, they were not strong.

> *Spiritual and relational vitality provide the strong root system that supports change.*

The congregation facing significant change must devote itself to its spiritual life and group cohesiveness. Even if you think your congregation is healthy in both areas, an increased emphasis on prayer groups, Bible study opportunities, and fellowship activities would be a wise move. These activities strengthen individual members and the congregation as a whole.

As we grow deeper, we can reach higher.

How Things Change

In going through some files recently, I came across a church newsletter from April 1976. It provided an interesting snapshot of this particular church at that time. This county seat Baptist church in a southern state was averaging over 650 in Sunday morning worship. What caught my attention was that they had only three full-time staff members! Today we talk in terms of a church needing one full-time staff member for every 100 worshippers. The same church today runs about 450 on a Sunday morning and has the equivalent of six full-time staff ministers. What changed?

A lot has changed in three and a half decades. Let me suggest five primary changes that affect churches, their staffing expectations, and their effectiveness in mission.

First, society has changed. In this particular case, what was once a small county seat town is now part of a metropolitan area made up not only of individuals commuting 45 minutes to an hour but of professionals and technical workers in locally situated medium-sized and large industries. Lifestyles have changed and people are busier with more personal and family activities. The community has a number of dynamic service, educational, and recreational organizations. Church participation is now just one of many options from which residents can choose.

Second, as a result of the first change, fewer volunteers are available to lead in programs, and those who do are often pulled to other activities as well. The church of 1976 included fathers who worked in the community, stay-at-home mothers, and a strong tradition of volunteer service. None of those things is true today. This is not meant to be negative, but it is a fact. People have more choices of where to invest their time and energy.

Third, the church scene has changed. Let's be honest: more competition exists between churches for members than existed three decades ago. Although we don't want to admit it, most churches are growing by transfer growth rather than conversions. This particular community at that time had one large Baptist church; now it has at least four large Baptist churches with multiple staff ministers. And the competition is not only between churches of the same denomination. A number of nondenominational churches in that community draw people of Baptist background, and

Although we don't want to admit it, most churches are growing by transfer growth rather than conversions.

22

believers seem more willing to consider other denominations when they seek a church home as well.

Fourth, congregations expect more of their ministers, perhaps due to the competition among churches. In the fast-paced media age in which we live, ministers must not only be competent but extraordinary. We expect to be "wowed" whenever they speak before the congregation, do leadership training, or initiate a new ministry. We want specialists in every area of church life—preschool, elementary, middle school, high school, college, young adult, singles, married young adults, median adults, senior adults, and so on. The stress this creates in the life of a minister is a downside of their service.

Fifth, an accepted church growth strategy is to staff for the growth you want and your church will "grow into it." This is not a bad concept, but sometimes a church staffs for numerical growth and the growth doesn't happen. Population shifts, emphases change, and the economy tanks, resulting in more staff members than the church can support and unwanted decisions about downsizing.

The primary challenge I would make to churches is to be realistic about where you are and what you can expect of staff leadership. Culture, people, needs, and methodologies have changed. Competent staff members want to address the issues of today and not those of yesterday in order to encourage church health. At the same time, they cannot do it alone. Church members must step up and accept responsibilities with the support of these professional staff ministers. There are some things that staff ministers can do and should do, but the church is made up primarily of lay believers, not professionals. The best staff members are both ministers and equippers, but the church needs those who are willing to be equipped.

The Importance of Innovation

During a recent workshop, participants began to question whether it was practical to take the time to initiate a new approach to leadership development in the church. Their concern was, "How can we attempt something new when we are dealing with basic survival in the church?" I shared my belief that a spirit of experimentation and innovation is key to the health of churches in the 21st century. We must move beyond maintenance to dreaming and planning for future opportunities. Said in another way, we must move from maintenance to mission.

> *Some of the seeds will prosper and yield new fruit. Some will wither and die.*

Afterward, I commented to one person that every church should have a Department of Research and Development. The church should always be trying new things. Of course, this is not easy. When things are going well in the church, people say, "Why bother to try something new?" When things are not going well, they say, "We don't have the time and resources to try something new."

Now I do not mean that we need a literal department with the name "Research and Development," but every church should be stretching itself by trying at least one new thing every year. This will institutionalize a spirit of innovation and anticipation. Perhaps it will be a new approach to leadership development such as Disciple Development Coaching© or a training program for Sunday school leaders. The innovation may be a new Bible study class that deals with contemporary issues or a spiritual formation group that encourages the practice of spiritual disciplines. I am not talking about big emphases that seek to involve all members of the congregation like Forty Days of Purpose. I am suggesting small, experimental initiatives that have the opportunity to nudge congregations in new directions without major changes in schedules, disruption of established programs, or a large allocation of financial resources.

This is "seed planting." Some of the seeds will prosper and yield new fruit. Some will wither and die. In any event, these innovations can generate new learning and a fresh appreciation for the church's ability to grow and adapt to meet the needs of the 21st century.

It's Not Broken Unless I Say It Is

In *The Practice of Adaptive Leadership,* authors Ronald Heifetz, Alexander Grashow, and Marty Linsky, write: "There is a myth that drives many change initiatives into the ground: that the organization needs to change because it is broken. The reality is that any social system (including an organization or a country or a family) is the way it is because the people in that system (at least those individuals and factions with the most leverage) want it that way. In that sense, on the whole, on balance, the system is working fine, even though it may appear to be "dysfunctional" in some respects to some members and outside observers, and even though it faces danger just over the horizon. As our colleague Jeff Lawrence poignantly says, 'There is no such thing as a dysfunctional organization, because every organization is perfectly aligned to achieve the results it currently gets.'"[14]

> *Change can only happen when that person or organization is ready to change.*

This goes a long way to help me understand why change is so difficult. If I am satisfied with my present situation, who are you to tell me that I need to do anything differently?

Change is not imposed on a person or an organization from outside. Change can only happen when that person or organization is ready to change. So what drives change?

- o Impending death. Although I know people who have been told they will die if they don't stop smoking, I have seen plenty of people who are ready to take off their oxygen mask for just one more puff. For most individuals and organizations, impending death is not necessarily a strong motivation to change because we cannot imagine the world without us or our organization.

- A "wake-up call." There is a sudden realization that disaster is on the doorstep: you can't make your mortgage payment, or there is no money to pay this month's salary checks, or the roof of the sanctuary just caved in and the insurance doesn't cover it. Few people can ignore disaster when it is staring them in the face.
- Embarrassment. When something happens that violates the values and standards of the individual or community *and* it becomes public knowledge, there is usually readiness to change. Whether it is a drunk and disorderly charge or abuse of a minor by a staff member, corrective action can no longer be delayed.
- Discontent. This is the least dramatic cause for change, but the one that may have the most lasting effect. When an individual discovers that he or she is underperforming or a church realizes unmet opportunities sit at its doorstep, this may well provide readiness for change. In such a situation, a perceptive member or a wise leader can cast a vision for a desired future that will provide motivation for life or organizational change.

Change rarely happens overnight but it will never happen without readiness for change.

Change and the Church

The old joke goes something like this. How many Baptists does it take to change a light bulb? The answer, "None. Why would we want to change anything?"

Change is never easy and rarely sought, but change is going to happen. We can either adapt to it or use it as a springboard for innovative and effective ministry. In his book, *Innovation and Entrepreneurship*, leadership guru Peter Drucker encouraged leaders to see changes around them as opportunities for purposeful and systemic innovation. He pointed out seven sources for innovation: the unexpected, incongruities, process need, industry and market structures, demographics, changes in perception, and new knowledge.[15]

Let's consider how those in congregational leadership might use these sources to make effective changes in the church.

First, the unexpected might be the unexpected success, the unexpected failure, or the unexpected outside event. Perhaps you begin a new worship service and people flock to it. Why is it a success—time, location, style, leadership? If we know why it works, perhaps we can apply the principles elsewhere. A new ministry may fail. Rather than just sweeping it under the rug, take the time to do a post-mortem and learn from the experience. An outside event like a natural disaster, a new business in town that brings in people from another part of the country or world, or an offer to purchase your property may be the catalyst for reassessment and repurposing of the church's resources.

> *Each church must decide what it does well, what it can do better, and what it offers to the community that no other group does.*

Second, the incongruities you encounter in your church may be the difference between an assumed reality and the actual reality. Your church may have a long history of reaching young adults through its college and single adult ministries so you continue to budget and staff for those ministries, but in reality, things have changed. Students no longer live in the local community but choose to commute long distances. The businesses that drew single adults have closed. Perhaps it is time to face reality and allocate those resources in new ways.

Third, the process that we used to do something may need to be changed. We already see this in the way that the church does publicity. We once depended primarily on print media—either done in-house or contracted out—to communicate with members, guests, and the community. Now we use digital media and less paper. What is the next thing that your church needs to discover as a better means of communication, information, or administration?

Fourth, although we hate to use the terminology, most church leaders realize that the religious "industry" and "market structure" have undergone major changes in recent years. We have seen

> *The church no longer occupies the same place in culture that it once did.*

the rise of megachurches (both denominational and non-denominational), house churches, and new expressions of faith (including many world religions) in our communities. People have more choices and they are exercising them. Each church must decide what it does well, what it can do better, and what it offers to the community that no other group does. This can provide new enthusiasm for creative ministry and new venues for your church to pursue.

Fifth, changes in demographics are both a challenge and an opportunity. As we discovered in recent Presidential elections, age, gender, and ethnicity have a tremendous impact on the electoral process. The church is not exempt from these changes. One significant change is in

> *New knowledge may provide us with new tools to communicate, lead, or educate.*

how we define family. Most churches are still programming for mother, father, and 2.5 children while the families coming through our doors (at least one time) are quite different. There are single parent families, blended families, and families where grandparents are raising grandchildren. The demographic reality calls for adaptation and innovation.

Sixth, the changes in perception, mood, and meaning that the church faces are often external. The church no longer occupies the same place in culture that it once did. Even for Christians, the church is only one part of a complicated lifestyle and may not even be in the top three places where one spends his or her time. We can see this as a negative situation or as an opportunity to help people redefine or rediscover the place of the church in their lives. Another change in perception affecting the church is the role of women in society. The church's response to the fact that women are more highly educated and increasingly prominent in secular leadership can be positive or negative. We can seize the opportunities this offers for a fresh wind of the Spirit to move in our midst or embrace a reactionary stance that stifles giftedness.

Seventh, we can use the new knowledge available to us to pursue new ministries or to be more effective in what we are currently doing. New knowledge may provide us with new tools to communicate, lead, or educate. All of the new knowledge is not equally useful, so we will need to be discerning in our evaluation of its worth, but we will miss a great resource if we ignore it.

Life brings significant changes to us as individuals; some are for the good and some challenge us to do something different. This is true for the church as well. What will your church do this year to address a changing world?

Questions for Reflection and Discussion

1. What is the attitude of your church and your leadership toward change? What's the most creative thing you have done as a church in the last three years?

2. Think about Drucker's seven sources for innovation. How does each apply to your church?
   - The unexpected—What has surprised us?
   - Incongruities—What is the difference between assumed and actual reality?
   - Process need—Is there a better way to do it?
   - Industry and market structure—What has changed about the community around us?
   - Demographics—What has changed about the people around us? How have we changed?
   - Changes in perception—What is the image of our church in the community?
   - New knowledge—What are some new tools that we need to use?

Chapter Four
Becoming Missional

Our God is a sending God who sent the Son to live among us. The Son, in turn, has sent us out to be His people and bear his message. Although this seems so simple, the church has often complicated the mission. Perhaps we can never embody the mission entirely, but we are called to move in that direction.

The God Who Initiates

One Sunday my pastor preached on the passage in Luke 15 about the loving father. Most of us call it the Parable of the Prodigal Son, but the primary emphasis is on the action of the father and, by implication, the action of the Heavenly Father.

The fresh insight I received that morning was that the father in the story took the initiative in reconciliation with both sons. First, when the younger son returned home, the father ran to meet the son without waiting for the son to approach him. Second, when the older brother refused to come in to the homecoming celebration, the father "went out and pleaded with him" (v. 28). The loving father was not passive but active in sharing love and grace with his sons.

> God is a sending God. Therefore, the church should be a sending church.

This text can help us to understand better the nature and mission of God as well as the nature and mission of the church. In the Hebrew Bible, we read that it is God who takes the initiative to redeem humankind. God sends messengers and prophets to inform and entreat the people of God to follow faithfully. In the New Testament account, God sends a Son to humanity to share the good news. God is a sending God. Therefore, the church should be a sending church. If it is God's intention to actively engage the world, then the church in carrying out the mission of God (*missio Dei*) must be a sending church.

This is the basis of a missional ecclesiology. "Ecclesiology" is simply the theological term related to the study of the doctrine of the church. "Missional" refers to the essential nature and vocation of the church as God's called and sent people. What's the difference between "missions" and "missional"? For many years, mission or missions was understood to be a program of the congregation supported by financial offerings, prayer, organizations, and projects. On the other hand, missional is a way of being and doing life (as individuals, groups, and congregations) that asks, "What does God want us to be, do, and become to continue the ministry of Christ within our own community and global context?" rather than "What do we want to be, do, and become to respond to our denominational programs or unexamined beliefs and traditions?"

In the missional congregation, mission refers to those initiatives individuals, impromptu groups, and organized entities take to respond to identified needs in the world, as a continuation of the mission of God. When a congregation adopts this understanding, it will gain a new perspective and set new priorities.

I believe that the adoption and practice of a missional ecclesiology can have a greater impact on Christian witness in the 21st century than the "emerging" or "emergent" church movement. In her book *The Great Emergence*[16], Phyllis Tickle makes a good case that the emergent movement will have more impact within denominations as it encourages Christians to learn about, honor, and practice some of the rich traditions of other "tribes." The emergent approach might be seen more as a tool for dealing with the postmodern situation we find ourselves in. On the other hand, a missional ecclesiology reframes the way we see who we are and what we are about.

How are we carrying out the mission of God? God has reached out to us and we, in turn, are to reach out to our world.

Some people seem to be a little tired of the term "missional church" and dismiss it as just another phrase tossed around by those who are unhappy with the way their church functions. This is a bit unfair. The idea that the church does not *have* a mission but *is* the mission of God in this world is a transforming concept. My concern lies elsewhere with those who assume that the only way to have a missional church is to disassemble the old church and start from scratch.

> *The idea that the church does not have a mission but is the mission of God in this world is a transforming concept.*

Many of the most popular books on the missional church make this assumption and provide numerous examples of those who have just left the established church and started something new. Their approach is that "it's broke, so don't waste your time trying to fix it." There is a place for such efforts, but I firmly believe that those of us who have cast our lot with the traditional church can work within its systems to help it become more missional.

Whose Are You?

The beginning point of becoming a missional church is to know *Whose* you are. You read that correctly. It is not as important for you to know who you are as a congregation—past history, present circumstances, and future possibilities—but to know the God who called your congregation into being.

> *The beginning point of joining God on mission is to acknowledge your dependence on God.*

Even if your church was birthed out of division and controversy, you are still the people of God and God has something prepared for you to do. The beginning point of joining God on mission is to acknowledge your dependence on God. The church does not exist primarily for its rituals, fellowship, or community involvement; it exists to be part of God's mission in this world.

If your church wants to become missional, you must begin with the central truth that without God, you can do nothing. The mission of God—*missio Dei*—is the life of the church. That is the beginning point.

Build Trust

A friend who raises funds for a theological institution has repeatedly pointed out to me the importance of relationships—whether you are dealing with individuals or foundations. "The best way to get funding from a foundation," he says, "is to know someone on the inside."

The same is true if you want to move a church toward being missional. You must build relationships and develop trust within the congregation, even if you are already on the inside. This can happen in several ways:

A priority is to find a champion. If you are the pastor or a staff member, the champion may be you. If you are not, seek to share the vision with the pastor or another ministerial staff member. This person will be part of staff discussions and will also be aware of the resources in the congregation—people, finances, facilities, equipment—that can be assets in the missional journey.

Second, you should not only make this a matter of prayer but seek opportunities to ask others in the church to pray for openness, opportunity, and receptivity to a missional mindset. This may be in Sunday school classes, committee meetings, or prayer services. This not only adds a spiritual dimension as you and others seek God's leadership, but it also makes others aware of the possibilities.

> *The Spirit of God often surprises us and pulls us in unexpected directions.*

Third, practice transparency and flexibility in this effort. Even if you have a vision of what your church might become, you must be candid and admit that you are not sure exactly how this may play out. The Spirit of God often surprises us (consider Philip and the Ethiopian eunuch) and pulls us in unexpected directions. Even the most committed leader does not have the full picture and needs to be open to new possibilities. People will trust you more if you exhibit openness to new ideas and approaches.

Fourth, find opportunities to give the vision away. The vision of becoming a missional church is not something to be hoarded but a treasure to be shared. As you do so, you not only bless others but the vision takes on new strength and vitality as others embrace it.

This may take time, but don't be concerned about a timetable. Transitions like this take place only when the people are ready to perceive God's mission.

Often we fail to act because we may know our ultimate goal, but we have not mapped out all the steps that will get us there. We understand and appreciate the need for our church to become more missional, but we can't articulate the plan that will lead us to the desired goal. We become bogged down in the details. The good news is that we don't need a well-thought-out plan to start the journey. It is more important just to do something!

Start Small

"Becoming a force of nature doesn't mean that all of our aspirations must be 'grand.' First steps are often small, and initial visions that focus energy effectively often address immediate problems. What matters is engagement in the service of a larger purpose rather than lofty aspirations that paralyze action. Indeed, it's a dangerous trap to believe that we can pursue only 'great visions.'"--Peter Senge, et al., *Presence: Human Purpose and the Field of the Future*[17]

Small steps can lead to great strides. Several years ago, Jessica Jackley, co-founder of KIVA.org, a micro-investment program, spoke at Willow Creek Association's Leadership Summit. In her interview with Jim Mellado, President of the WCA, she said, "Don't be afraid to start small." KIVA's founders didn't apologize for starting with just seven entrepreneurs. Jackley pointed out that you can talk all you want about an idea, but once you begin and actually do something—even if it's small—people respond to you differently. The best way to create big change is to have the patience and attention to focus on one particular area and to serve that area as well as you can.

> *"Don't be afraid to start small."*

Where is a good point to start in your church? The beginning point may be acknowledging in some way those who are already actively involved in ministry in the community even if it is not an "official" church ministry. Another possibility is to start thinking about putting more time into people development (coaching, mentoring, instilling spiritual disciplines) than program development. Perhaps it involves getting the staff to read and discuss a book on what it means to be a missional church. It may mean identifying one thing the church is doing that is no longer needed and invest that time and energy into a new outwardly-focused ministry.

Our initial efforts may not show remarkable success but at least we will be moving in the right direction. We may make mistakes, but we may also discover the Spirit of God speaking to our congregation in a special way.

Build on Your Strengths

> *Each church is uniquely gifted to do something in its setting that no other church can do, or at least, do as well.*

For years we have talked about the uniqueness of every individual and the fact that "God has wired each of us" in a certain way. As a result, we have made efforts to help individual believers discover their gifts, passions, and personality types in order to serve more effectively. Is this idea also true for the church as well?

Marcus Buckingham is the author of several ground-breaking books including *First, Break All the Rules*[18] and *Now Discover Your Strengths.*[19] While he was with the Gallup Organization, he helped develop the Strengths-Based approach to management. The basic idea is that we should spend more time using the abilities we already have than trying to improve upon our deficits or weaknesses.

Out of that conference came the idea that this may be the best approach for churches to pursue as well. Contrary to the Natural Church Development approach[20] of discovering where your church falls short ("where it leaks" in NCD terminology), a church would be better off to accentuate its unique strengths.

How does this apply to the missional church? Each church is uniquely gifted to do something in its setting than no other church can do or, at least, do as well. Due to your location, facility resources, the gifts of your membership, and the abilities of your leadership, you can address a community need or develop a ministry for which your church is uniquely gifted.

How do you do this? Two things are essential. First, pray to find and be open to the leading of God's spirit. This must be

open-hearted, no-holds-
barred praying. Second,
engage in purposeful
conversation among church
members. This involves
ongoing, face-to-face

> *We must be willing to give up the old in order to embrace the new.*

dialogue among everyone in the church. Of course, both of
these activities take time, but it will be time well invested if the
church can come to appreciate its strengths and discern how
to use them effectively.

Discover Your Assets

The mindset of many established churches is to maintain
the most visible of their assets—people, property, and
programs—without digging deeper to discover the rich
resources that may be available just below the surface. There
are people in every congregation whose abilities are not being
used. In *Growing an Engaged Church*, Albert Winseman
suggests that disengaged church members may just be
seeking the right place to serve. He writes, "If you want to
grow a spiritually healthy, vibrant, dynamic congregation,
focus on increasing the engagement level of your members."[21]

To engage such people, however, we need to a new
mindset. Rather than thinking about how we can "use" them (a
rather selfish approach) in the established work of the
congregation, we may need to think in terms of how to
empower them to start new ministries or to commission them
to serve as missionaries to the community.

Many programs in the church are "sacred cows" that have
outlived their usefulness. Perhaps, however, they can provide
the seeds for a new or improved ministry. We must be willing
to give up the old in order to embrace the new.

Churches should also consider how to use their physical
resources in missional endeavors. Most traditional churches
have large facilities that are used only a few hours a week.
Some have chosen to rent portions of their facilities in order to
generate income. The most effective use of these facilities,

however, would be to create new ministries to occupy that space or partner with already established community programs to strengthen their work.

A tool that churches can use to assess what they have available for Kingdom work is Asset-based community development (ABCD).[22] This methodology seeks to uncover and utilize the strengths within communities as a means for sustainable development. If undertaken as a community process and not limited to church members, ABCD can open doors for new engagement with the community around the church. In fact, there may be those outside the church who can become part of the team to address needs.

God has blessed us in many ways, although we may not be fully aware of those blessings or how to use them most effectively.

Get Outside the Walls

An interesting thing strikes me about the early church. Much of what they did was in very public places such as the city square, the marketplace, and the Temple. Early Christians did not have buildings, so they were out among the people, interacting in the everyday flow of life.

> *Early Christians did not have buildings, so they were out among the people, interacting in the everyday flow of life.*

Those of us who are believers today need this same type of involvement. If we hope for our churches to become more missional, we need to get outside the walls and get to know our communities.

I had lunch with some friends in another city recently, and they decided to take me to (what we call in middle Tennessee) a "meat and three" restaurant. The place was not fancy, the food was good, and the people were friendly. While we were eating, one of my friends commented, "These folks are very different from those who come to our church on any given Sunday." This was very perceptive. He noted that most of the people who attended their church were of a particular social and economic class; there was not a lot of diversity. The realization provided fresh insight about their particular church, who it reached, and possibilities for change.

We need those "Aha!" moments. Most of them will come only when we take ourselves into different, often unfamiliar, environments. We can drive a different route to work, eat at a new restaurant, or seek out invitations to various civic groups. Whatever we do, we must be intentional about getting outside of our normal routines to begin to understand what God is about in the world.

I believe that those of us who are church people are called to be both gathered and scattered. We gather to worship, learn, and encourage one another, but then we need to scatter around our community. When we do that—keeping our eyes, ears, and hearts open—we will start becoming more missional.

Questions for Reflection and Discussion

1. Who should be on your "becoming missional" team? Why?

2. What small experiments can your church try that would make a big difference in its ministries?

3. What are your church's strengths? Its gifts? Think beyond facilities and location to people and relationships.

4. How can you open your eyes to undiscovered assets both within and outside the church?

4. If you got some church members together for a "road trip" to interact with people who are not like them, where would you go? How would you debrief? What scriptures might inform your reflection?

Section Two
Leadership Lessons

I learned a long time ago that I know a lot more about leadership than I practice. Over the last four decades, I have been responsible for everything from a supply platoon in the U.S. Army in Vietnam to a state-wide ministry with some twenty-five employees and a budget of over a million dollars. As I think back, I got some things right and some things wrong.

What did I get right? A couple of things come to mind. Even when I was a youngster, my Dad (who was an enlisted man in World War II) told me that I should remember two sets of initials—RHIP and RHIR. RHIP means "rank has its privileges." RHIR stands for "rank has its responsibilities." In Reserve Officers Training Corps in college, I was taught that an officer always takes care of his men first (please remember that this was before there was much gender diversity in the ranks). For example, an officer makes sure his troops are fed and housed before he takes care of his own needs. This approach stayed with me in ministry positions as well. I made sure I never asked anything for myself that was not available to everyone on the staff—training opportunities, compensation, and vacation. I also made every effort to ensure that our department staff received the same benefits others in the organization received.

Second, I did a pretty good job of building a staff team wherever I served. By my estimate, over 90 percent of my hires were good ones, borne out by the fact that most of those people continued to work there and do a good job long after I left. Hiring decisions are the most important ones any leader can make, and I learned that I was headed for trouble if I did not invest considerable time, energy, and prayer in those decisions.

What did I get wrong? There is probably not enough space for that list, but let me identify two things. First, although I think of myself as a rational decision-maker, too many of my decisions were made by intuition. In an effort to show progress, I occasionally chose a path that was risky or untried. Sometimes this worked and sometimes it didn't, but too often such decisions wasted time and resources. In a couple of situations, I only escaped a catastrophe by the grace of God! If I had the opportunity to do it over again, I would take more time on some decisions or seek more counsel.

Second, and this amplifies on the observation above, I too often operated from a "lone ranger" mentality. I think I took the saying, "It's lonely at the top," too seriously. When I worked for a state Baptist convention, one of the great resources available to me was other staff members in various departments in the building. I did more "drop in" visits with other department leaders than most of my colleagues, but I know now that I would have been better off if I had done more of this and in a timelier manner. Just because one has been placed in a leadership or managerial position, he or she should not fail to use the experience and skills of others both inside and outside the organization.

Although some people may be born leaders, I think most of us spend a lifetime developing the skills it takes to be a competent leader. If we are honest with ourselves, the task is never complete.

If a leader seeks to move a church to become more missional, she or he will learn some valuable lessons along the way. Some will come only from experience, but the leader can begin the process through self-assessment and an awareness of the resources at hand. In this section, we will consider some of the ways to align one's leadership for a missional ministry.

Chapter Five

What Kind of Leaders Does the Missional Church Need?

Even a casual study of Scripture makes clear that in order for churches to become missional, they need different kinds of leaders. God called people with different abilities and gifts to lead the church as new opportunities emerged. The Bible contains few position descriptions, but we do find many examples of men and women who were willing to respond to that call at just the right time.

> *Both within and outside of the church and its structures, we need apostolic leaders.*

Apostolic Leaders

When we think about apostolic leadership, our attention usually goes immediately to the Apostle Paul—out there on

45

the cutting edge, starting new faith communities, facing hardships, and winning Gentiles to the Way. In *Missional Renaissance*, Reggie McNeal reminds us that Paul was not the only apostle, and there was more than one style of apostolic leadership.

In comparing the Pauline and Petrine styles, for example, he notes: "Some find that they can be missional only in new settings and are quite at home engaging cultures that are not culturally Christian. Other leaders are most comfortable and effective at home serving as missionaries to the church culture, challenging those in it to connect with the Spirit's agenda in the world beyond them."[23]

While Paul was penetrating the Gentile world with the gospel, Peter and James stayed in Jerusalem and shared the message of Christ in the center of Jewish influence. They were confronting an established system with a message of renewal, but their mission was still apostolic.

Both within and outside of the church and its structures, we need apostolic leaders. Those who function within the church are leaders who realize that just as God is a sending God (sending forth God's own son), the church is a sending church. The church should always be looking outward to engage the culture, but someone may have to remind it to do so.

Those who work outside the walls to engage the culture get a lot of attention, but we must not neglect those who work in church and judicatory structures to lead their constituents in the process of becoming missional. More of us will find ourselves in that role than as missional entrepreneurs.

McNeal goes on to point out others besides Paul and the eleven who were also apostolic leaders—Lydia, Stephen, Onesimus, Barnabas, the unnamed Ethiopian official, Timothy, Luke---each worked in a unique way either within or outside the established religious structures to further the gospel.

If you are an apostolic leader, where is God calling you to serve?

Improvisational Leaders

For some time I have struggled with my aversion to the term "strategic planning" and the idea of a "strategic planning process." Part of my discomfort has come from being exposed by Alan Roxburgh to the idea of "discontinuous change." I don't think that I do any harm to Roxburgh's presentation to summarize it as "everything tied down is coming loose." Where we once thought linearly, assuming that the future would be like the past,

> *None of us knows what tomorrow (or this afternoon) holds.*

and planned accordingly, reality has shown us that this is not the way things are. The unexpected happens (the Internet, 9/11, the Iraqi war, financial chaos) and all of our great plans go out the window.

So what are we to do? In an article in *Christian Century*, writer Jason Byassee refers to something Sam Wells wrote in *Improvisation*. Byassee writes, "Sam Wells takes this metaphor further . . . [when] he argues that Christian living is like improvisational acting rather than script-based acting. Players practice intensely in order to be able to react to the unexpected on stage. No two acts of improvisation are ever alike, just as no two acts of Christian faithfulness are. Preparation allows for improvisation, and so for faithfulness."[24]

Whether we are living the Christian life or leading a Christian organization, we are really improvising. None of us knows what tomorrow (or this afternoon) holds. Does this give us permission to be sloppy and just take what comes our way? No. Actually it demands that we strengthen our relationship to God, recognize and hone our strengths, and be prepared for the unexpected. I have heard some people talk about a person who "just had dumb luck" and stumbled into something good. If we examine the situation closer, we often discover that the good fortune was more than happenstance. The person involved was ready to seize the opportunity that came his or her way, much like the actor who said it took him twenty years to become an "overnight success."

Wells' observation encourages us to be prepared by knowing who we are and understanding our relationship to God. The unexpected will certainly happen! God calls us to faithfulness in such times of uncertainty.

Functional Leaders

In response to my observation on a blog that leadership in the church is an art rather than a science, my friend Stephen Currie made this comment: "I'm beginning to wonder what 'leading' even means for Jesus' followers. Jesus told us that the Gentile leaders rule by lording over their subjects, but for his followers, this should not be. He who leads will be 'the slave of all'. There are many of us who feel lost in the church if we are not 'leading' in some way. So yeah, I think leading-by-serving is an art. The people who have modeled this best for me were not men and women of learning . . . they just did it for the love of serving as Jesus did."[25]

Stephen makes a good point. For one thing, his comments remind us that "leadership" is more than a role or a title. Every group of human beings will have leadership of some type, but it is conferred in many different ways. Leadership may be assumed, usurped, negotiated, or bestowed, but it is there. Leadership in the church is different because it is governed by the way God made us.

In most organizations we find two primary types of leadership. We can call them different things, but basically there are leaders

> *"Leadership "is more than a role or title.*

with titles and leaders without titles. Simply putting someone in a leadership role does not make that person a leader. Just ask the young pastor who has been called to what is commonly called a "family-sized congregation." The pastor may assume that he or she is the "leader" of that church, but church members really know who the leader is—a matriarch or patriarch who has been around for awhile and is related to most of the church members in some way.

In the early church, leadership seems to have been more of a function than a title. In reading about the church at Jerusalem, we learn that a number of people who were "servants" of the church—such as Stephen and Philip—also became gifted spokespersons for the Christian faith. Barnabas was first recognized for his generosity and sense of caring before he was delegated the job of envoy to the church at Antioch. While there, other gifts of leadership became evident and led to his role as a missionary.

> *Any person who exercises his or her gifts as a servant of the church is a leader.*

The early church had a charismatic leadership characterized by a gifting from God for the various functions it needed. Function was more important than title. As Paul pointed out in 1 Corinthians 12, there are different functions in the body, but all are necessary and none is more important than any other.

Perhaps we define "leadership" too narrowly. Any person who exercises his or her gifts as a servant of the church is a leader—the greeter as well as the Sunday school teacher; the children's worker as well as the pastor; the custodian as well as the administrator. In the final evaluation, the title or the role is not as important as faithfulness to God and God's people in exercising our gifts. This is servant leadership.

Lay Leaders

Baptists in the South, along with mainline churches such as Methodists, Presbyterians, and some others, once prided themselves on their lay religious education programs. They emphasized that the "church school" was not just for children and youth but for adults as well. Baptists offered opportunities for laity to take "study courses" based on books that covered everything from Bible survey to Sunday school growth methodology.

How are we equipping lay people for church leadership today? In reality, most of our churches are not. I am not calling for a return to the "Church Study Course," but I do think this is a neglected area in many of our churches. We do a good job of Bible teaching but little to equip lay leaders.

As we think about this challenge, let me share a few observations about the adults we have the opportunity to equip for ministry. Some of these are based on my experience in leading a couple of lay learning experiences in our church. They are not meant to be perceived as positives or negatives but as factors to consider in the intentional formation of lay leaders.

First, they are well educated, many with college degrees and management and leadership training in their companies and communities. Many are avid readers. They know good training when they see it.

Second, they are digitally connected. Although they may not be in love with technology, they are exposed to it on a regular basis and many are adept at using it. This skill is not limited to young adults; this is true of many adults of all ages.

Third, they are busy people, with many demands on their time—work, community service, family, and the logistics of "doing life" like shopping, housework, home repair, paying bills, and so forth. Carving out time for something else is not easy.

Fourth, they come from various denominations. Many people who have become lay leaders in your church probably did not grow up in your faith tradition. In leadership classes I have led in our church, I have found a number who grew up in other faith groups. Again, this is not a bad thing and may even be a blessing!

Fifth, their family situations vary. Some are part of the traditional "Mom and Dad, three kids, and a dog" kind of family, but others are in a second marriage, have blended families, are single parents, have never been married, or are single adults caring for aging parents.

Sixth, they are open to new relationships. One of the most significant byproducts of a leadership training experience can be bringing people from different generations and walks of life together. In churches of any size, large or small, it is quite common that people don't know each other. They know their Sunday school classmates or those with whom they work on various projects, but their sphere of involvement is limited.

Seventh, they are seeking spiritual insight for their lives. Many adults hunger for a place where they can share their deepest needs without judgment and find spiritual guidance. This may sound like a simple thing, but most adults have to search to find this type of community.

Equipping adults as lay leaders for the 21st century church is one of the most significant opportunities open to us today. The task will require our best thinking and ample resources of people, time, and money.

Women Leaders

Several years ago while I was working for a state Baptist convention, I received a phone call from a woman who had recently accepted the call as pastor of a church that participated in the convention. She was about to attend her first annual meeting of the convention. After receiving a less than hospitable welcome from the local Baptist association, she was concerned about her messenger credentials being challenged on the floor of the convention. Someone had suggested that I might walk her through the constitution and bylaws and identify any mine fields. We had a pleasant conversation, and she thanked me for my guidance. My response was, "Don't mention it. In fact, please don't let anyone know that we talked." Not my finest hour and certainly not a "profile in courage."

> *Many adults hunger for a place where they can share their deepest needs without judgment and find spiritual guidance.*

The results, at least, were positive. She did attend the convention, was introduced as a new pastor, and experienced no problems to the best of my knowledge.

About five years ago, I was visiting with a friend who was associate pastor of an African-American church in our area. She was actively seeking ordination and the opportunity to pastor a church. Her national denomination would soon be meeting in her city, and I asked if she planned to attend. She responded very quickly, "I don't go where I am not accepted and respected."

> *What can the average Baptist Christian do to empower women to discover and use their gifts in ministry?*

She did become a senior pastor shortly afterward, but she had to move to another denomination first.

Juxtaposing these two conversations, separated by about twenty years, helps me to reflect on how women who are called to ministry respond to their circumstances and what it means to the denominations that birthed them.

In the first instance, I believe that the pastor who went to the state Baptist convention was acting out of hope (perhaps with her church's encouragement) that the system could change and that women would be welcomed as pastors in a traditional Baptist convention. Eventually, this woman found that this was not going to happen and she left to join another Baptist group. But she tried.

My friend of recent years had invested herself in a traditional Baptist denomination, pushing the edges of acceptance, and had finally come to the same conclusion. She moved on.

What does this say to us about the possibilities for women in ministry today? First, I believe it says that we still have a long way to go. Even moderate Baptist churches who voice support for women ministers are slow to consider them as "senior" pastors—that is, the person who preaches from the pulpit and is head of staff. Second, the lesson is that there are alternatives for women called to preach. They may have to leave and join a more progressive Baptist group or another denomination in order to fulfill their calling, but the option is available.

Both of these observations create some frustration for me. On one hand, moderate Baptists are making progress, but it is painfully slow. On the other hand, moderate Baptists lose out when our gifted women must leave the churches that nurtured them in order to live out their calling.

At least I am grateful that both of the women I know have gone on to fruitful ministries, but I am sad for those they left behind.

What can the average Baptist Christian do to empower women to discover and use their gifts in ministry? Let me suggest several things.

First, support organizations that speak for women. Baptist Women in Ministry[26] has taken a bold step in employing Pam Durso as the organization's first full-time executive director. BWIM has a solid reputation of connecting, resourcing, and advocating for women in Christian ministry. They need our personal and financial support to continue this important work.

Second, discover organizations that challenge women to a world vision of service, especially those that relate to women and family issues—poverty, maternal care, sexual trafficking, and similar concerns. One such organization is Global Women[27]. Cindy Dawson, her staff, and board are making remarkable progress in creating global friendships among women for shared learning and service. They are also providing valuable resources for local churches.

Third, encourage women who are seeking to live out their ministry passion. You will find these individuals locally, nationally, and internationally. One of these people is Becky Sumrall, executive director of Christian Women's Jobs Corps of Middle Tennessee[28]. She has built an organization that provides women "a hand up, not a hand out." CWJC helps women to develop skills and embrace values in order to attain a better life for themselves and their families. Such organizations are found in many other states as well.

Another person who comes to mind is Suzanah Raffield, a young woman with a global vision who helped women of the Kidetete Women's Cooperative in Tanzania to develop a microenterprise that will raise the standard of living for their families through their own initiative and diligence. Suzanah is representative of a number of young women who are making a difference in the world by pursuing their calling to serve and minister.

Fourth, find a young woman in your church who has been called to ministry and provide encouragement for her. One way you can do this is to point her toward places of service where she can discern and develop her gifts for ministry. Passport Camps[29] and student.go[30] offer young women the opportunity to serve in settings that respect their calling and giftedness. Introduce her to college and seminary programs that welcome women who are called to ministry.

> *Calling out and empowering young leaders is a painful process, both for the young leaders and the church!*

Fifth, when your church has a staff vacancy, take the initiative to talk to the search committee or seek the resumes of qualified women as well as men for the position. This includes the role of pastor. As a male I think I have the privilege of saying that I would rather have a competent woman than a mediocre man as my pastor any day! Let's raise our sights and look at the female candidates who are ready to serve in every leadership role in the life of the church.

Young Leaders

As Christian leaders, we often say that we want to nurture a new generation of leaders and involve them in the life of the church. On several occasions, however, I have personally observed questioning and criticism of the decisions and leadership of young adults who have been asked to assume responsibilities in the local church.

Although the desire is sincere, too often the reality is that we are too set in our ways, uncomfortable with change, and want everything to be "perfect" (according to our standards). Calling out and empowering young leaders is a painful process, both for the young leaders and the church! They will never be ready unless they try, succeed, and sometimes fail. In *Missional Renaissance*, Reggie McNeal points out that "Jesus deployed his disciples long before they were ready."[31] From personal experience they learned how much more they needed to learn from the Master and were motivated to do so.

"I just don't belong here. I can't find a place to plug in at this church."

In order for young adults to become leaders, they need three things.

First, they need a chance to serve. They need opportunities to accept responsibilities that are meaningful and consequential. When I was 23 years old, I was a platoon leader in the U. S. Army. I was responsible for the care of at least 30 people and at least a million dollars' worth of equipment. Of course, I was under authority, but I was also accountable. Can you imagine this happening in the church?

Second, they need champions. Young adults need older leaders who will be advocates on boards, committees, and staffs to actively seek out, employ or enlist, and empower young leaders. These individuals keep their eyes open for talented young leaders and find places for them to serve.

Third, they need coaches. Young leaders do have much to learn and a teachable spirit is important. At the same time, they probably already know more than they are being given the opportunity to practice. Young leaders need persons who will stand alongside them, help them to set goals, and then hold them accountable to pursue those goals.

If we are sincere about wanting younger leaders in our churches and organizations, we must carve out a space for them.

Developing a Culture of Leader Empowerment in Your Church

One of the most discouraging things a pastor or staff minister can hear is this: "I just don't belong here. I can't find a place to plug in at this church." This may be the last conversation the minister will have with this person, and the person may say it as he or she walks out the door of the church on Sunday morning.

The person's perception may be true. Because of the direction a particular congregation has chosen to pursue, the gifts and talents of this individual may fall outside the opportunities for service and fellowship offered there. However, it is more likely that the failure to connect has more to do with the way a church empowers its members than with the lack of opportunities available.

Ephesians 4:11-13 offers a model for equipping and empowering believers: "So Christ himself gave the apostles, the prophets, the evangelists, the pastors and teachers, to equip his people for works of service, so that the body of Christ may be built up until we all reach unity in the faith and in the knowledge of the Son of God and become mature, attaining to the whole measure of the fullness of Christ."

Some believers are set aside for the purpose of equipping God's people for the "works of service" so that everyone can find his or her place in the Body of Christ and grow in Christlikeness. This does not mean that we have two levels of giftedness—the clergy and the laity, for example—but different functions in the body of Christ. Those we usually refer to as "clergy" are ministers and those we call "laity" are also ministers. Those gifted as apostles, prophets, evangelists, pastors, and teachers (the last two may be one function) are specifically charged to equip and empower others for ministry.

So how do those with the responsibility to equip and empower other believers do their work? They do it by developing a culture in the church that fulfills the goals of equipping and empowering. Here are some specific actions that contribute to this type of culture.

- The church must recognize all gifts without respect to gender, age, or ethnicity. This means that women, older adults, median adults, younger adults, youth, children, and people of various races all have a part to play in the church. We must remove the prejudices and ingrained habits that are barriers to their service.

- We must encourage people to discover how God has "wired them up." Each person is a unique mixture of spiritual gifts, talents, experiences and passions. When we understand who we are, we are better prepared to find the right place of service.

- The church must organize for equipping and empowerment. What are the structures—discernment, counseling, assessment, training, placement—that we can put in place to help people use what they have to further the ministry of the church?
- We must find the methodology to measure our progress and determine how effective we are in the process of equipping and empowerment, although this is not easy. As someone said, "What gets measured gets done."

- We must train both "clergy" and "laity" to mentor and coach each other to use their giftedness and find the right placement in the Body of Christ. Scripture offers many examples, especially in the work of Barnabas and Paul.

God continues to call gifted and talented men and women for "works of service." We must be more intentional about helping them find how to perform that service.

Questions for Reflection and Discussion

1. Do you know an apostolic leader, one who is on the "cutting edge" of ministry?
How would you describe that person's gifts, skills, and abilities?

2. What are some of the more creative ministries in your community? How can your church partner with them as you become more missional?

3. What is your church's strategy for calling out and equipping leaders—lay persons, women, young adults, and youth?

Chapter Six
Discovering Your Calling

What's your calling? I think more Christians are becoming aware that they have a calling even if they are not clergy. The observation that "believer's baptism is our ordination to ministry" has taken on new meaning for many people in the pew as they have rediscovered the concept of "vocation" as a personal calling from God.

As individuals discover their calling or vocation, they are also becoming aware that not every person fulfills his or her calling within the faith community. In *Growing an Engaged Church*, Albert Winseman points out that "there are far more opportunities to discover one's calling outside the walls of the congregation or parish."[32] I think he is saying that our calling does not necessarily have to be in a traditional place of service within the congregation.

Winseman suggests that there are three questions spiritual leaders need to ask to help believers turn their dreams or inclinations into callings:

What are your talents or strengths?

What do you love to do?

If time and money were no object, what would you do for God?[33]

What are Your Talents and Strengths?

Have you ever seriously considered the assumptions that Christians embrace in their church involvement? These are things that we have picked up along the way. It is unlikely that they have been adopted as church policy or even specifically taught, but they have become ingrained in our psyches. Over the years, I have observed a couple of interesting assumptions that Christians seem to have embraced.

> *Putting a person in the wrong place of service does not help the person or the position of service!*

First, if I enjoy doing something, then it is not "God's will for me." This may come from all the testimonies we have heard about ministers "struggling" with their calling. Or it may be a result of the idea that God doesn't really want us to enjoy ourselves and demands self-denial. We might summarize this as "If I feel good about it, obviously it is the wrong thing for me to do." This says a lot about our concept of God, doesn't it?

Second, there is the idea that there are some things in the church that anyone can do. For example, "Anyone can be a greeter. How hard is it to say hello to people and give them an order of worship?" Well, for some people, meeting absolute strangers is an agonizing task (and don't think that the strangers don't realize it when they encounter such a person). Putting a person in the wrong place of service does not help the person or the position of service! It certainly does not contribute to spiritual growth.

In *Growing an Engaged Church*, Albert Winseman cites research that "individuals have the most room for growth in their areas of greatest talent."[34] He argues that when we take an individual's talents and strengths seriously, we can unleash great human potential.

> *We should not make excuses about what we are not gifted to do but accept the challenge to use what we have.*

This should not be so surprising for Christian leaders. Throughout the New Testament, we read of people who were specially gifted for the work they did. They were not called to "positions" but to "ministry" that grew out of their God-given gifts. We also read about people who had developed certain talents over the years—artistic, musical, organizational, etc.—and used them for God's work. Paul's training in Greek philosophy and his skills as a tentmaker serve as examples.

People in our churches today have such skills or natural inclinations. These are valuable resources for ministry, and individuals are often pleased when asked to share them in Christian work.

This "strengths-based" approach affirms that God has created each of us as unique individuals with great capacity for growth and service. We should recognize that there are areas where we may not be gifted, but why expend time and energy on trying to work on those things and not using what God has already given to us? We should not make excuses about what we are not gifted to do but accept the challenge to use what we have.

Rather than wishing for more, let's learn to discover and use what we already have.

What Do You Love to Do?

The question is so simple that it seems ridiculous that we do not ask it more often in the church: "What do you love to do?" We recognize that God blesses each person with spiritual gifts, and we appreciate the talents that people have discovered and nurtured over the years. The major motivating factor in a person's life, however, is what they are passionate about.

If one has a passion for an activity, he or she will alter their schedule, make sacrifices, and commit to do what needs to be done to be involved. A friend invited me to a pro football game recently. We sat outside in chilling temperatures with snow flurries coming down to watch a team with a mediocre record. Why? Because we care about the sport.

> *We may never know the source of passion, but we can tell when a person is passionate about something.*

What is the source of passion? The sources are as diverse as people are unique. Perhaps it is the result of an almost forgotten childhood experience shared with a parent or friend. Maybe it comes from studying under a teacher or working with a mentor who embodied excitement about a subject or a task. For believers, it is always a possibility that the Spirit of God has spoken though worship, Scripture, testimony, or hands-on experience.

We may never know the source of passion, but we can tell when a person is passionate about something: the person's eyes widen, their voice is a little louder and more animated, and their step is a bit more energetic. We observe an enthusiasm we do not normally see in that person. In fact, the Greek origin of the word enthusiasm is "being possessed by a god." Something special has been added to the situation.

In the church, we can discover those things that give members passion by both asking and listening. First, simply asking, "What do you love to do?" and then listening carefully, without judgment, and without preconceived ideas.

If we can discover what a person is passionate about, we will have made a major step in helping that person discover his or her calling.

No Limitations

How do you measure success? For many, it is a nice house, functional car(s), and a well-stocked refrigerator and pantry. Just to have these things makes us richer than the majority of people in the world. Of course, we don't stop there. We would like our share of electronics, opportunities to eat out on a regular basis, a few "toys" (name your favorite), and a variety of entertainment options. If we are a bit more introspective, we will share our desire for personal health, good family or friend relationships, a challenging vocation, and a growing relationship with God.

> *"If money and time were no object, what would you do for God?"*

If I asked you to prepare a list of things that make one successful, you would pretty quickly come up some of the things I have already noted. In doing this exercise, we describe our preferred reality, the type of life we work to create despite economic downturns, sickness, catastrophes, and relocations. There is nothing inherently wrong with this, but this perception of reality can become a box that limits us from becoming what we might as followers of Christ.

In *Growing an Engaged Church*, one of the questions that Albert Winseman suggests that spiritual leaders should ask congregants is, "If money and time were no object, what would you do for God?" I have used this question in a number of different settings with various audiences over the years. If the audience is made up of well-established median adults, I often pick up puzzled reactions and cynical remarks like, "Well, it's a little late for that!" But I have also seen skeptical looks on the faces of young adults when I have asked this question of them. They have already picked their "box" (or had it picked for them by parents or respected leaders) and are busy reinforcing it. One group that is often energized by the question is older adults who are about to retire or have already retired, but perhaps it is because they have built up some resources and have the flexibility to try something new!

No matter their age each believer needs to ask himself or herself this question from time to time as a reality check—where am I, how did I get here, and is this where I really want to be? This provides us the chance to reflect on whether the life we are living is the one that best honors God and uses our gifts for God's service.

One of most memorable statements by Martin Luther King, Jr., was "I have a dream." King's dream was a reality check for people in the 1960's who still struggled with the place of African-Americans in society. The dream was not based on financial or temporal resources but a preferred future for all Americans—no matter their race or status in society. We continue to be challenged by that dream.

Have you lost your dream of following God's calling? I encourage you to recover it.

Questions for Reflection and Discussion

1. If you took seriously the statement that "believer's baptism is your ordination to ministry," what difference would it make in your life?

2. What are you passionate about? How can you use that passion to serve God?

3. If money and time were no object, what would you do for God?

4. What opportunities are provided in your church for individuals to consider the answers to these questions?

Chapter Seven

Leading in the 21st Century

What's at the Core?

In the recent past, the leadership of organizations was built on a mechanistic model. There was a clear organizational chart, decisions flowed from the top down, and responsibilities were codified in job descriptions. The primary responsibility of each succeeding level of supervision was to make sure that those individuals at the level below were doing what they were hired to do—nothing more and nothing less. This mechanistic model stifled creativity, meaning, and relationships for everyone except (perhaps) those at the very top.

The new organic model of leadership is built on a core of spirituality and relationships. When the leadership team of the Union Baptist Association in Houston began seeking to create a way to lead churches in transformational change, they realized that spiritual and relational vitality was the driving force for church transformation. They also realized that they needed to model it themselves as a team if they were going to guide churches in transformational change (see Jim Herrington, et al., *Leading Congregational Change*).

> *The new organic model of leadership is built on a core of spirituality and relationships.*

Spiritual and relational vitality are two dimensions of a single reality Christ taught in this way: "One of them, an expert in the law, tested him with this question: 'Teacher, which is the greatest commandment in the Law?' Jesus replied: '"Love the Lord your God with all your heart and with all your soul and with all your mind.' This is the first and greatest commandment. And the second is like it: 'Love your neighbor as yourself.' All the Law and the Prophets hang on these two commandments" (Matthew 22:35-40).

If a congregation or judicatory does not have both a commitment to a spiritual walk and healthy relationships at its core, it will neither survive nor prosper. Even a secular organization must have both core values that look beyond itself and vital relationships among its people if it is going to be something other than a machine.

> *Spiritual and relational vitality form the basis for effective leadership in the 21st century.*

Spiritual and relational vitality form the basis for effective leadership in the 21st century. Why? Because people are looking for meaning and they want to be valued for who they are. If these basic needs are not met, the organization is dead in the water. How are you developing spiritual and relational vitality in your setting?

Pathfinding

One Saturday several years ago, I spent an afternoon helping my grandson, Noah, prepare for an oral report on

Davy Crockett, the Tennessee frontiersman, hunter, politician, and popular hero. We even went to iTunes and downloaded "The Ballad of Davy Crockett" from the 1950's TV series.

> *Every group needs someone who is out there on the cutting edge.*

Although Crockett's adventures may not have opened up new territory like Daniel Boone, Jim Bridger, Kit Carson, John Fremont, and other pioneers, he was something of a pathfinder, discovering new trails and hunting lands in the rapidly changing Tennessee wilderness. Men like Crockett were always just one step ahead of civilization. They prepared the way for expansion into new territories.

We still need pathfinders today. As we consider what makes effective organizations in the 21st century (churches, judicatories, etc.), we have to name "pathfinding" as one of the key values of such organizations. Every group needs someone who is out there on the cutting edge, scouting out new possibilities and identifying resources that allow the organization to address those opportunities. In the 18th and 19th centuries, scouting parties were sent out ahead of settlers to find not only the best places to live and work but the resources for a viable settlement there.

Effective organizations today must embrace this value. In industry, this function is often assigned to a research and development department, but many companies have discovered that the best innovations come from the factory floor or even from the user of the product. Whether your organization is a church or judicatory, each person should receive a coonskin cap and become a pathfinder, looking for new opportunities and new resources. This requires giving each person some time to explore or dream, just to wander around.

Such exploration may involve reading, research, benchmarking (discovering what others are doing), talking to constituents, or just speculating. Leaders in effective 21st century organizations will fight for this "blue sky" time because it is the only thing that will keep their organization vital and effective.

Inherent in this mental model is the idea that the organization will be on the move. It will not be in the same place tomorrow that it is today. Even if the organization wants to stay in one place, it cannot because the environment around it is changing. In order to serve in that new environment, the organization must seek out new ways to serve within it.

Once you have found the path you wish to follow, how do you get everyone onto that path and moving forward?

It's a risky task, but it can also be a lot of fun!

Aligning

Super Bowl commercials can either be memorable or outrageous (or both). I don't remember the product or service, but my favorite was one that appeared several years ago. The commercial featured several cowboys on horseback attempting to "herd cats." I suppose I liked it because it was so familiar—anyone in a leadership role has found that working with a group of independent-minded people is often like herding cats! It is difficult to get all of them going in the same direction.

Another task an organization in the 21st century must do is to align team members and constituents in such a way that they are all pursuing the same goal. Once you have found the path you wish to follow, how do you get everyone onto that path and moving forward?

This assumes that everyone is motivated to some degree and actually moving. I believe a law of physics states that it is easier to change the direction of an object in motion than to put a body at rest into motion. Most people have something they want to accomplish in life or in your organization, but it may have nothing to do with the goal the leadership has in mind.

I used to do a non-verbal exercise with groups that went something like this. I would ask the group to stand in a circle and lock arms. Then I would ask each person to pick a place in the room where he or she wanted to go and to move the group to that point. Of course, this involved a lot of pulling and pushing. The smaller members of the group were pulled in different directions by competing larger members. Usually, the pulling and tugging resulted in the circle being broken and one section of the group pulling away from the others. In debriefing, I often asked, "How would this have been different if you could have talked with each other?" After discussion, someone would comment, "Well, we could have negotiated, set priorities, and taken the group to everyone's spot eventually."

I think it was Peter Senge's writing that introduced me to the idea of alignment.[35] The basic idea is that everyone is going somewhere, but is there some way to get everyone either to put aside or alter their goals so that everyone can move in the same direction, at least for a short while? Very often an individual's goal can even be seen as a means of attaining the larger organizational goal so that it is a win-win situation.

This type of alignment requires clarity of purpose, listening, and negotiating. It may even require compromise (not a dirty word and the way that our government moved forward before we became so polarized in certain positions). Alignment does not mean that I give up sincerely held values or beliefs, but it does mean being willing to walk in the same direction with colleagues in order to reach the goals of the organization.

> *The leader must learn how to truly empower individuals.*

This is hard work, but if it were easy, anyone could do it!

Empowering

A leader was addressing a group and commented, "It is our

goal to find each person's spark of creativity and to water it."
Unfortunately, that mixed metaphor often describes the task
that leaders of churches and other organizations embrace!
The word "empowerment" is not in their vocabulary.

One of the key leadership characteristics of the leader of a
21st century organization is empowering. The leader must
learn how to truly empower individuals. Each person has
unique gifts, skills, and abilities. An effective leader will help
individuals discover those attributes and release them for use
in the work of the organization. The leader's role is more than
saying, "You can do this," but to give responsibility, resources,
and space for the participants to act.

This is not simply helping persons discover their gifts so
that their names can be penciled into boxes on an
organizational chart. It is much more in keeping with what
Myron Madden called "the power to bless." We see this Old
Testament theme most clearly in the experience of Jacob and
Esau. One was blessed by the father and one was not.
Blessing involves affirmation, encouragement, and
empowerment.

One of the greatest dangers of being part of any
organization—including the church—is losing one's self-
identity in the larger group. Every group of human beings has
a tendency to push for conformity and solidarity. When an
outlier pops up, he or she is usually brought back into line. An
effective 21st century organization balances the concepts of
unity and uniformity. The leader wants everyone going in the
same direction (alignment) but he or she also respects the
unique gifts of each person (empowerment).

Of course, once a person discovers his or her unique
calling, the leader may recognize that person does not really
fit with the mission of the organization. In such a situation, the
leader may have to "push the young bird out of the nest" so he
or she can fulfill their calling. This is not done with malice but
with a desire to help the person find where they can best
serve.

Empowerment is a highly relational aspect of 21st century leadership, but it is not the only one.

Coaching

When March Madness comes upon us, coaches take center stage more predominantly than in many sports. When we think about coaches, we picture nicely dressed men and women yelling, sweating, and throwing tantrums on the sidelines of college basketball games. At the same time, these coaches show that a certain passion is involved in the art of coaching. They encourage young men and women to stay the course to achieve a goal, and that is what coaching is all about.

> *Coaches are people who walk along beside others and help them attain their full potential.*

Those who lead organizations in the 21st century will have to exercise a coaching function. Coaches are people who walk along beside others and help them to attain their full potential. Like the characteristic of empowering, coaching is a highly relational matter. A coach establishes rapport with the client, helps him or her determine an action plan and agenda, and then holds the individual accountable for his or her actions. This is a dynamic and interactive process; along the way, the plan will have to be revised as the individual faces reality (much as a basketball coach in the final minutes of a close tournament game makes last-minute changes in the game plan in an attempt to get a few more points on the scoreboard).

Although I have never been an athlete, I have had a number of coaches. A couple started out as mentors (individuals who could teach me some things I needed to know) and turned into coaches (persons who helped me to determine a course, pursue it, and make course corrections as necessary).

In an organization or a church, the skill of coaching goes hand in hand with the skill of empowerment. In sports, the coach doesn't play the game; the athlete does. If we believe in the equipping ministry of the church (Ephesians 4:11-12), we will see the ministry of coaching believers as essential to the building up of the body of Christ.

> *Sharing knowledge is essential to the 21st century organization.*

Although there will be some in the 21st century church who want to be told what to do, there are many more who want to discover the task that God has called them to and simply want someone to walk alongside them as they attempt to do it.

Networking

"Networking" has become a common term among individuals—especially entrepreneurs—who are attempting to connect with those who can help them achieve their business plan and those who are potential customers. Networking is also an essential skill for leaders of 21st century organizations.

Peter Senge has explained the importance of internal networkers or community builders in developing learning organizations. He describes such people as "the seed carriers of the new culture, who can move freely about the organization to find those who are predisposed to bring about change, help out in organizational experiments and aid in the diffusion of new learnings."[36]

If you have a 20th century perspective on leadership, this characteristic of leadership will really get under your skin. If you are part of an organization or judicatory, you may not see the value of encouraging the "gadfly" employee who flits from desk to desk, cubicle to cubicle, or office to office looking over other employees' shoulders. If you are a church leader, you may be suspicious of the staff member or lay person cruising the hall with a cup of coffee in his or her hand, stopping to talk with whoever walks by, and peeking into Sunday School classrooms. Either of the above descriptions may not be the most effective way to share information within your organization or church, but there must be a mechanism for this to happen. Sharing knowledge is essential to the 21st century organization.

Many people call this the sharing of "best practices"—here's what works for us. The person who shares a best practice is not guaranteeing that if you adopt this practice in your setting that you will have the same level of success. He or she is simply reporting, "This is how we solved our problem. Maybe it will help you to solve yours."

In some way, networking needs to be institutionalized within the organization or church. Encourage both planned and unplanned gatherings of persons representing different parts of your organization. Both organizations and churches might do better if everyone had the opportunity to stop by a common coffee or snack area before retreating to their individual cubicles or classrooms. Finding ways to encourage people from different parts of the organization to cross paths—such as a common entry or fellowship area—might be helpful. Meetings of leaders could focus more on sharing from the participants rather than dissemination of information from the upper echelons.

> *Paul was surrounded by a team of gifted individuals that was continually changing.*

Good things happen in every community—church, judicatory, or business. We just need to find ways to "scatter the seeds."

One word of warning: This will only work if you are willing to take some risks. Notice that Senge used the words "change" and "experiment" above. A 21st century leader who adopts this approach must be willing to put up with a little messiness and occasional flat-out chaos. When you encourage people to share their creativity, you may be surprised, amazed, and unsettled. That's one of the risks of 21st century leadership.

Beyond the Local Church

How do these skills[37] apply beyond the local church in the work of judicatories or denominational structures in the 21st

century? I think we see a valid biblical model for this approach.

When we think of the work of the apostle Paul, we tend to focus on him alone. In reality, Paul was surrounded by a team of gifted individuals that was continually changing. We know the names of some of them—Barnabas, Luke, Timothy, John Mark, even Priscilla and Aquila. At various points, different individuals became part of the apostolic team led by Paul. The composition of the group evolved and changed over the years. Very often members came on board, made their contribution to the work of encouraging churches in an area, and then attached themselves to a particular church or churches to continue their work apart from Paul. Some were already mature and gifted persons when they joined the Pauline team, but others were nurtured by the apostle and the group. How did this team practice the functions we have been discussing?

First, they were certainly pathfinders. From the day that Paul and Barnabas left the church at Antioch, they were on new ground for the gospel. Sometimes it was fertile, sometimes it was stony, and sometimes it just needed to be cultivated. Throughout Paul's ministry, he took his team into new and potentially hazardous situations to share the gospel and establish churches, thus taking the Christian church into new territory.

Second, when it comes to alignment, "herding cats" is easy compared to the task of bringing together Jews and Gentiles, slave and free, male and female, rich and poor in order to focus on the spread of the gospel. The Pauline team often embodied within itself a cross-cultural element that helped find ways to get everyone going in the same direction.

Third, Paul and his associates were all about empowerment. I would like to think that this is one thing Paul learned from Barnabas. Paul himself was a pretty rough stone before Barnabas took him under his wing. Paul continued to develop new leaders both within the team and in the churches. The Pauline team was not going to stay in one place very long, so it was necessary to call out, train, and empower indigenous leadership.

Fourth, we know that Paul provided coaching to church leaders and others because we have letters he wrote (or dictated) to local churches dealing with specific situations and needs. Sometimes this guidance was very directive in nature, but he often challenged those in the church to take responsibility for themselves and deal with issues within their fellowship. Coaching also took place as he sent team members to deal with troubled churches and leaders.

Fifth, Pauline team members were the "seed carriers" or networkers of their day, going from church to church and sharing news of how the gospel was making progress in various cities. At one point, Paul developed a network of giving churches to provide assistance for the church at Jerusalem when it was in financial need, but we also see the networking function in the sharing of letters among churches and the constant visits of Paul and his team.

I am not saying that the Pauline team had a checklist of these five functions, but I am saying that they embraced a relational, organic, and fluid approach to ministry leadership described by these functions that is very appropriate for our day. As we leave behind the mechanistic, bureaucratic leadership models of the 20th century, this approach provides a new mental model for doing ministry.

In an article in *The Christian Century*, mission strategist Ray Bakke was quoted as saying, "Almost 90 percent of the barriers hampering urban ministry are found in the church's own ecclesial and mission structures."[38] I don't know the source of this statistic, but his statement does challenge us to find new models for ministry leadership for churches and judicatories in the 21st century. This more organic approach is one of them.

Questions for Reflection and Discussion

1. How do you encourage spiritual and relational vitality in your church?

2. Identify people you know who exhibit these skills:

    Pathfinding
    Aligning
    Empowering
    Coaching
    Networking

3. How are they using these skills in Christian service?

Chapter Eight

Developing an Effective
Leadership Team

The talents of many people are needed for a church to become more missional. A key move is to assemble a leadership team that can work together to lead the church to accomplish this task. In order for such a team to be effective, each member must play his or her role. In working with church staff teams, I suggest that the following assumptions are necessary to developing an effective staff team:

- Every staff member can make a unique contribution to the staff team.
- An effective staff team benefits the church it serves.
- An effective staff team helps each staff member develop his/her ministry gifts.
- An effective staff team requires mutual commitment.

- An effective staff team requires intentional leadership.

Contributing to the Team

At the Cooperative Baptist Fellowship General Assembly in Tampa several years ago, Molly Marshall, Anita Flowers, and I led an Essentials conference on "Developing an Effective Leadership Team." The participants came ready to learn and the energy in the group was good. Those of us who facilitated the sessions shared some ideas, but we learned as well.

In order for a team to be effective, each member must play his or her role.

This is an important topic. Most organizations including churches and not-for-profits are led by teams. Many young adults are naturally drawn to the opportunity to work with others in a team setting. Older adults may have had negative experiences in teams that cause them to resist being part of a team; they may have some unlearning to do to be good team members. The effective functioning of the leadership team may well determine the success or failure of the entity; therefore we should spend more time developing effective leadership teams. In order to do so, we need to embrace several basic assumptions.

The first assumption is that every staff member can make a unique contribution to the team. Notice I said that every staff member "can" make a contribution; this does not guarantee that each staff member will. Several things must occur for the team member to contribute.

The effective functioning of the leadership team may well determine the success or failure of the entity.

The team member must want to be part of the team. He or she must make a conscious decision to be a contributing member of the group. Neither threats nor material rewards can force or motivate this response. Wanting to be an integral part of the team is an internal decision each member makes.

The team member must understand the mission of the team. Confusion about what the group is supposed to accomplish leads to uncertainty about where the team is going and the role the team member is expected to play in the process.

The team member must fit the team. No matter how much the person wants to be part of the team or understands the mission, if the "fit" is wrong, then the team will not succeed. Patrick Lencioni talks about "getting the right people on the bus." This means that their gifts, abilities, and commitments fulfill some need of the team. If they don't have what it takes to make a contribution, they need to find the place where they can be of more use to themselves and others.

Effective teams are made of people who want to be part of the team, know what is expected of them, and feel that they are in the right place at the right time. When all of this happens, the stage is set for each member to contribute. As 1 Corinthians 12:7 states, "Now to each one the manifestation of the Spirit is given for the common good."

Benefiting the Church

Effective leadership teams don't exist for themselves; they exist to benefit their church. A team may enjoy being together and encouraging one another, but if they fail to serve the church, then they have failed. Effective leadership benefits the church in a number of ways.

First, the leadership team can help the church to achieve its mission. Of course, this assumes that the church knows what its mission is! If the church does not know its mission, perhaps the initial way a team can serve the church is to help it discover and articulate that mission.

Leaders are always seeking possibilities and encouraging others to discover them as well.

Second, they work with members of the church to identify and pursue the actions that will move it toward its mission, always being sensitive to the context in which the church finds itself, its resources (both known and undiscovered), and the intervention of the Spirit.

Third, an effective leadership team equips persons as they seek to achieve the mission. A leadership team should not be expected to do it all themselves. They must constantly be discovering

> *"If you take care of your people, they will take care of you."*

and equipping persons for ministry both inside and outside the walls of the church. This action multiplies the work of the team and insures the continuity of the church.

Fourth, the leadership team is responsible to be good stewards of the resources placed at their disposal. These include people, finances, property, equipment, and even digital resources. This responsibility is not just to the people of the church but to God as well.

Fifth, perhaps the greatest contribution a leadership team can make is to dream and challenge members of the church to dream. Leaders are always seeking possibilities and encouraging others to discover them as well.

In these and other ways, an effective leadership team is a blessing to its church.

Developing Team Members

Since each team member brings unique skills, gifts, and talents to a leadership team, he or she should not only be called upon to contribute those to the work of the team but be encouraged to develop them further. An effective leadership team provides a place where each member can both serve and grow and the church usually provides challenges that foster that growth.

The development of team members requires a significant investment of resources, so why should the church or organization take the initiative to encourage such development? There are several good reasons.

First, a staff member who is valued will be more engaged. In his book *The Dream Manager*, Matthew Kelly points out that the real challenge for any organization is not turnover but engagement.[39] If someone is appreciated and effectively engaged, that person will not only stay with the organization but will be motivated to do his or her best.

Second, if a staff member is respected and his or her personal development is encouraged, he or she will want to give back. Kelly says, "If you take care of your people, they will take care of you." When individuals know that they are appreciated, they want to reciprocate.

Third, as we develop "value-added" team members, we will add value to the church. As we model personal development for team members, we are affirming our desire that every member of our church or organization will seek to achieve their full potential in Christ.

This personal staff development can take a number of forms. The supervision provided each team member should embody this concept of development as well as service. Intentional team building will facilitate the growth of each team member. The church must also be committed to providing the resources for ongoing learning experiences—educational materials, conference and seminar participation, coaching and mentoring, and formal degree programs.

Someone may raise an objection to this approach: "What if they become so good that they outgrow us?" This is a valid point, but an opportunity for the church to realize that it is part of the Kingdom of God. Perhaps one of the church's opportunities is to equip and encourage leaders who will be able to invest their capabilities elsewhere and benefit other believers. For an organization, whether it is faith-based or not, the opportunity to build leaders has immediate benefits but may result in its corporate culture being spread elsewhere as those leaders find other places of service.

Building Team Commitment

As I began planning a workshop on team development, I

contacted a number of pastors and church staff members and asked for observations about their own teams. Here are two of the responses I received:

"Our church staff team just doesn't get along!"
—A pastor in Georgia

"We just don't seem to be on the same page."
—A church staff member in Tennessee

> *The most effective teams are those in which members recognize their own strengths, their styles of communicating, and where they need help to be more effective.*

Such responses indicated to me that an effective staff team requires mutual commitment to specific values and principles. Team members must have a core around which they can grow, encourage each other, and serve their church or organization. The statement is made in *Leading Congregational Change* that "Spiritual and relational vitality [provide] the life-giving power that faithful people experience together as they passionately pursue God's vision for their lives."[40] If a team is going to come together, they must build on a spiritual and relational core.

Spiritual vitality comes from several things. First, there must be an acknowledgement that each member of the team is a child of God, gifted by God, and called by God to ministry. Second, the team must be committed to times of corporate worship. This is most effective when team members take turns in leadership, offering some of their own insights and gifts to the experience. Third, team members must pray for each other on a regular basis, both in team meetings and between meetings.

Simply working together on common tasks does not guarantee relational vitality. The most effective teams are those in which members recognize their own strengths, their styles of communicating, and where they need help to be more effective. The use of profiles like PeopleMap, DiSC, or

Clifton Strengths Finder[41] can facilitate this discussion, but they are only the beginning point for ongoing dialogue and learning. Effective teams also make the time to fellowship and play, thus exposing other attributes of their personalities as well as their interests. Effective teams also "cover" for each other from time to time, reducing the stress that a member may be under due to personal or family circumstances.

The development of spiritual and relational vitality doesn't just happen in a team but must be intentional. This requires planning and commitment but the results are worth the effort.

Leading an Effective Team

An old management axiom goes, "What gets counted gets done." The idea behind this is that we are intentional about those things we know are going to be measured. With rare exceptions, nothing worthwhile happens unless someone works to make it happen or chooses to become its "champion." This is true for effective leadership teams as well.

The desire for an effective team begins with a person. This is usually the pastor or executive director of the organization but it may be a team member, a member of the board, or a church member. If the initiative does not come from the leader of the team, he or she must not only buy into the concept but thoroughly embrace it. The leader models the idea, nurtures its development, and intervenes to assure its survival.

Although the leader does not give up his or her leadership responsibility to the church or the organization, he or she will have to leave ego at the door and adopt the roles of advocate, facilitator, mentor, and coach. The leader is still an essential part of the team because of the gifts that he or she brings to the table but, Max DePree says in *Leadership Jazz*, the leader becomes part of the jazz ensemble rather than the conductor of the symphony.

The most rewarding aspect of developing an effective leadership team is that, if it is done well, then the team members themselves will become its supporters and champions. As they see the value of being part of this type of team, the team members will contribute to its success. They will come to appreciate the opportunities for growth, service, and ministry such a team provides.

Questions for Reflection and Discussion

1. How much time does your staff team spend in staff development? What form does it take? Who plans this time?

2. Do you have a staff covenant? Do you review it on a regular basis?

3. What is the unique contribution you make to your staff team? How did you discover what you can contribute?

4. What do you need from other team members?

Afterword

Will We Know the Future When We See It?

First Chronicles mentions the people of Issachar "who had understanding of the times" (12:32) and were able to instruct Israel what to do. Wouldn't it be a blessing to have such a gift—to be able to understand exactly what is going on in our time and discern the right path to follow? Occasionally we see persons with this gift in business, government, or the church. These individuals seem to be able to understand not only what is "trending," but what is important to pursue in order to assure a successful future.

Not everyone has the gift. Many people, in an attempt to prove that it is hard to predict the future, point to a statement (perhaps apocryphal) attributed in 1943 to Thomas J. Watson, chairman of the board of International Business Machines: "I think there is a world market for about five computers." Although few may have the gift, there are some actions that we might embrace in order to catch a glimpse of "the next big thing" that will change society or empower the ministry of the church.

First, we can keep our eyes and ears open. Leaders need to be exposed to new and even controversial ideas. This means reading outside your field, especially publications like Fast Company[42]. Browsing through and listening to TED Talks[43] is also very stimulating and encourages creative thinking.

> *Leaders need to be exposed to new and even controversial ideas.*

Second, we can learn from others and ask a lot of questions. When Patrick Lencioni's consulting company begins working with an organization, they go in with a blank slate—they have done little or no research and they come asking questions. They want to provide what the organization needs rather than sell what they do. Don't be afraid to ask questions that provide clarity and insight. The only "bad" question is the one you did not ask.[44]

Third, we must value what has worked but not hold it too tightly. Everything was new and innovative at one point from the pipe organ to the rotary-dial telephone. Although some things—inventions, processes, and programs—endure and are adapted over time to maintain their effectiveness, others need to be given a respectful funeral. We can give thanks for what has served us faithfully, but we must recognize when it is time to move on.

> *The only "bad" question is the one you did not ask.*

Fourth we must be willing to experiment and experience. Before we commit too completely to a new idea, try it out in small ways or visit places where it is being done. When I was involved in a building program several years ago, the architect suggested that we use a new type of floor covering. A wise member of the committee asked, "Is there some place where this has been used for awhile that we can visit?" We will want to try things for ourselves, but we can also learn from others' experiences.

Fifth, we can play with possibilities. Before we get too deep into the planning process or implementation phase, we should take a step back, see if the pieces can be arranged differently, or ask if there are other ways to approach this that we have not considered. An idea may be the "hot item" right now, but is it something that promises to endure over time?

Although the origin of the quote is not clear, this statement has a lot of truth to it: *"The best way to predict the future is to invent it."* We help to create the future for our organizations by the choice of what we will embrace and encourage. I pray we will have the wisdom of the people of Issachar in doing so.

After the Afterword

This little volume is not meant to be the last word in the conversation about becoming missional, only the contribution of one individual who loves the church and wants to see it be all that God intends for it. As I talk with church leaders—both clergy and laity, colleagues, and seminary students, I continue to gain new insights about this process and celebrate what the people of God are doing under the leadership of God's spirit.

I welcome you, the reader, into this conversation. Please feel free to contact me through Pinnacle Leadership Associates at ircelh@pinnaclelead.com. You can follow Barnabas File, my blog, at www.barnabasfile.blogspot.com. My Twitter address is @ircel. I welcome your comments and critique.

I also encourage you to take advantage of the consulting, coaching, and training opportunities offered by Pinnacle

Leadership Associates. You can learn more at www.pinnaclelead.com.

"Now to him who is able to do immeasurably more than all we ask or imagine, according to his power that is at work within us, to him be glory in the church and in Christ Jesus throughout all generations, for ever and ever! Amen."— Ephesians 3:20-21

Ircel Harrison grew up in the church and loves it, but he believes that God is not through with the church because of the new challenges and opportunities that God continues to provide. Harrison has been a campus minister as well as a denominational worker and has served in practically every position available in a Baptist church. He is coaching coordinator of Pinnacle Leadership Associates and supplemental faculty in Ministry Praxis at Central Baptist Theological Seminary. He and his wife, Rita, live in Murfreesboro, Tennessee. He may be contacted at ircelharrison@gmail.com.

Endnotes

[1] Alan Roxburgh, *Introducing Missional Church*, and Lois Barrett, et al., *Treasures in Clay Jars* for example.

[2] Valley Forge: Judson Press, 2009.

[3] *Coming Together in the 21st Century*, Kindle location 1760.

[4] *Coming Together in the 21st Century*, Kindle location 1795.

[5] *Coming Together in the 21st Century*, Kindle location 1803.

[6] *Coming Together in the 21st Century*, Kindle location 1827.

[7] San Francisco: Jossey-Bass, 2009, p. 62.

[8] *Missional Renaissance*, p. 92.

[9] *Missional Renaissance*, p. 93.

[10] *Missional Renaissance*, p. 45.

[11] *Missional Renaissance*, p. 104.

[12] HarperCollins Publishers, 2011, p. 134.

[13] Herrington, et al. *Leading Congregational Change*. Read more about this in Chapter Seven.

[14] Boston, MA: Cambridge Leadership Associates, 2009, p. 17

[15] HarperCollins, 2009.

[16] Grand Rapids, MI: BakerBooks, 2012.

[17] New York: Currency Doubleday, 2005, Kindle location 1943.

[18] Buckingham, Marcus, and Curt Coffman. *First, Break All the Rules*. Simon and Schuster, 1998.

[19] New York: Gallup Press, 1999.

[20] Christian A. Schwarz, *Natural Church Development: A Guide to Eight Essential Qualities of Healthy Churches.* Saint Charles, IL: ChurchSmart Resources, 1996.

[21] *Growing an Engaged Church*, Kindle Location 673.

[22] For more information on Asset-Based Community Development, see Luther K. Snow, *The Power of Asset Mapping: How Your Congregation can Act on Its Gifts* and Cameron Harder, *Discovering the Other: Asset-Based Approaches for Building Community Together.*

[23] *Missional Renaissance*, p. 132.

[24] http://www.faithandleadership.com/multimedia/samuel-wells-improvising-leadership?utm_source=conceptpage&utm_medium=principle&utm_campaign=transformativeleadership, accessed March 11, 2014.

[25] Personal e-mail from Stephen Currie.

[26] www.bwim.info

[27] http://www.globalwomengo.org

[28] http://www.cwjcmiddletn.org/

[29] http://www.passportcamps.org/2009/home/index.html

[30] http://www.studentdotgo.org/

[31] *Missional Renaissance*, p. 106.

[32] New York: Gallup Press, 2006, Kindle location 799

[33] *Growing an Engaged Church*, Kindle location 800.

[34] *Growing an Engaged Church*, Kindle location 763.

[35] *The Fifth Discipline: The Art and Practice of the Learning Organization.* New York: Doubleday Business, 1990.

[36] *The Leader of the Future.* San Francisco: Jossey-Bass Publishers, 1996, Kindle location 972

[37] The skills of pathfinding, aligning, and empowering were suggested in an article by Stephen Covey in *The Leader of the Future*. As mentioned above, Peter Senge's description of the networking function was presented in another article in the same book. For more on coaching, see Tidsworth and Harrison, *Disciple Development Coaching* (Nurturing Faith Press).

[38] Jason Byassee, "Emerging in Seattle," The Christian Century, February 24, 2009.

[39] Hyperion Books, 2007, page 2.

[40] Herrington, et al., San Francisco: Jossey-Bass Publishers, 2000, Kindle location 286.

[41] For information on the PeopleMap, contact Pinnacle Leadership Associates at www.pinnaclelead.com. For information on the DiSC Personal Profile system, contact Ircel Harrison at ircelharrison@gmail.com. The Clifton Strengths Finder link can be found in several publications including Winseman, et al., *Living Your Strengths*, New York: Gallup Press, 2008.

[42] http://www.fastcompany.com/

[43] http://www.ted.com/

[44] http://astore.amazon.com/barnfile-20/detail/0787976393

Made in the USA
Charleston, SC
30 October 2014